Aviation Elite Units

Jagdgeschwader 51 'Mölders'

Aviation Elite Units • 22

Jagdgeschwader 51 'Mölders'

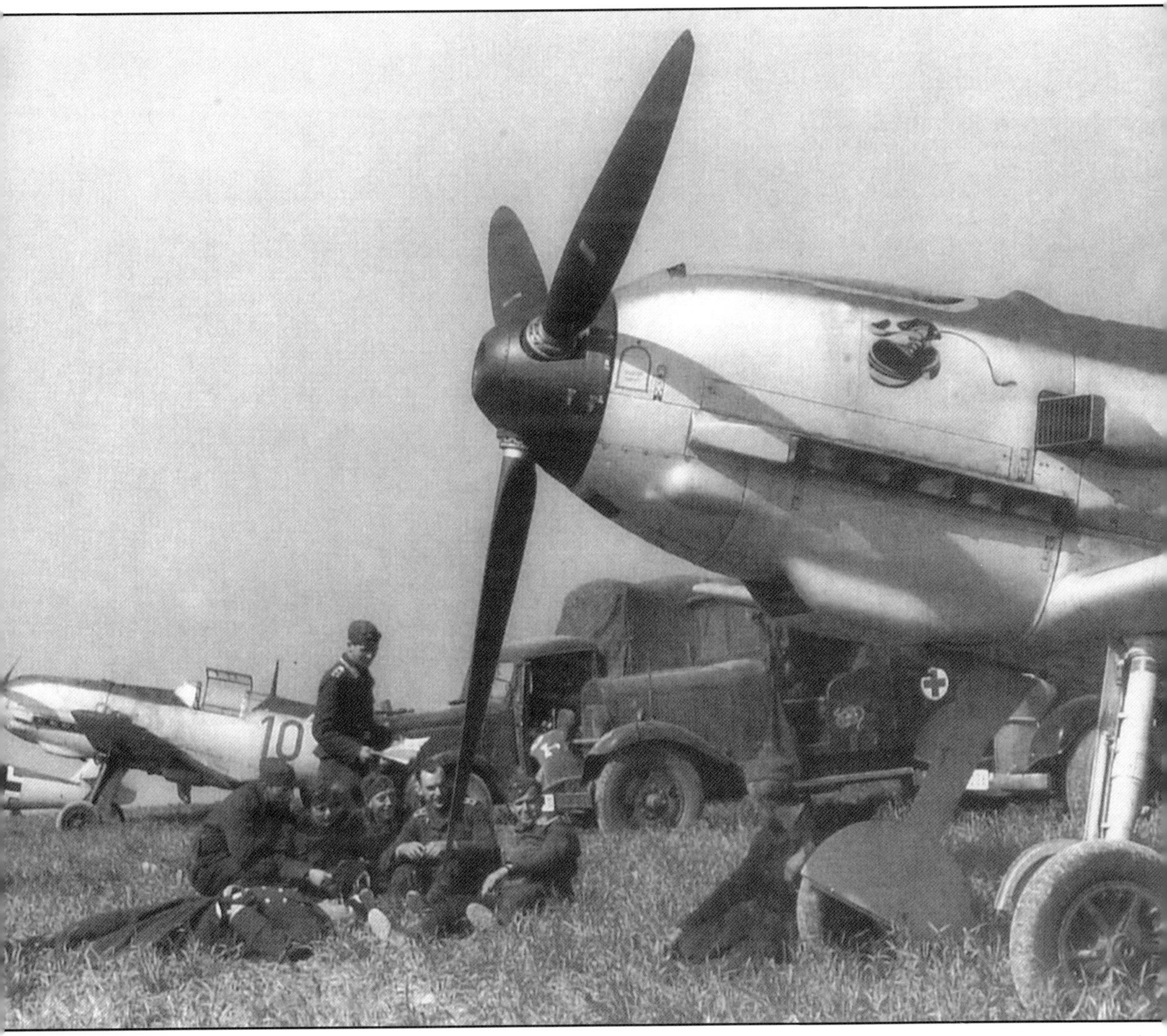

John Weal

Series editor Tony Holmes

Front Cover
It was shortly after 1400 hrs on 6 September 1940 when Major Werner Mölders, *Kommodore* of JG 51, lifted off in his Bf 109E from Pihen/St Inglevert – the base which the *Geschwaderstab* shared with Hauptmann Brustellin's I. *Gruppe* for much of the Battle of Britain. The weak early autumn sun had long since burned off the last traces of ground mist clinging to Pihen's grassy surface a short distance inland from Cap Gris Nez, but a light haze still persisted over the Straits.

The yellow rudder of Mölders' *Emil* was decorated with 32 kill bars. The first 25 of these had been scored during his previous service with JG 53, while the last three represented a trio of Hurricanes brought down in the space of little more than ten minutes northeast of Folkestone just six days earlier.

Now Mölders and his wingman, Oberleutnant Georg Claus, were heading for the same area of the Kent coast for another *freie Jagd* sweep. But this time pickings were fewer, and the *Kommodore* was able to claim only a single (unidentified) Spitfire over Folkestone – victory number 33 out of the final total of 101 that would be credited to the pilot many consider to be the greatest Luftwaffe fighter leader of World War 2 (*Cover artwork by Mark Postlethwaite*)

First published in Great Britain in 2006 by Osprey Publishing
Midland House, West Way, Botley, Oxford, OX2 0PH
443 Park Avenue South, New York, NY, 10016, USA
E-mail: info@ospreypublishing.com

CIP Data for this publication is available from the British Library

ISBN: 978 1 84603 045 1

Edited by Tony Holmes
Page design by Mark Holt
Cover Artwork by Mark Postlethwaite
Aircraft Profiles by John Weal
Index by Alan Thatcher
Originated by PPS Grasmere, Leeds, UK
Printed and bound in China through Bookbuilders

08 09 10 11 12 11 10 9 8 7 6 5 4 3 2

ACKNOWLEDGEMENTS
The author would like to thank the following individuals for their generous help in providing information and photographs – Peter Baines, Alfred Bieler, Wilhelm T Goebel, Manfred Griehl, Rolf Hase, the late Hans Langer, Walter Matthiesen, Gerhard Nolte, Axel Paul, Tomás Poruba, Dr Alfred Price, the late Frank Schermerhorn, K H Schmeelke, Jerry Scutts and Robert Simpson.

EDITOR'S NOTE
To make this best-selling series as authoritative as possible, the Editor would be interested in hearing from any individual who may have relevant photographs, documentation or first-hand experiences relating to the world's elite pilots, and their aircraft, of the various theatres of war. Any material used will be credited to its original source. Please write to Tony Holmes via e-mail at: tony.holmes@zen.co.uk

CONTENTS

FORMATION AND PHONEY WAR

Many of the early fighter pilots, both Allied and enemy, who survived World War 1 subsequently went on to serve their countries once again in World War 2.

Most of those who chose, and were selected, to remain in the services during the intervening years (which, for the German veterans, would mean first being accepted into the 100,000-man standing army permitted by the post-World War 1 Treaty of Versailles, and then transferring to the covert air arm of the Weimar Republic before the emergence of the Luftwaffe proper in 1935) had risen to high rank and positions of authority, and command, by the outbreak of World War 2.

In contrast, the majority of those who had opted, or had been obliged, to return to civilian life in the aftermath of the first conflict, but who then answered their country's call to arms by rejoining the ranks upon the outbreak of fresh hostilities in September 1939, often fought their second war from behind humbler desks.

Very few from either category managed to get back on operations and fly combat missions in both world wars. Fewer still claimed ace status in both conflicts, and were honoured in each with the highest decoration their nation could then bestow. One such, however, was Theodor Osterkamp.

A youthful Theodor Osterkamp perches on the wheel of his Fokker D VIII in Flanders in the late summer of 1918

One of Osterkamp's pre-war commands was II./JG 134, which he activated on 15 March 1936. Here, in full parade uniform, complete with early-pattern steel helmet and bouquet of flowers tucked into his brocade waist-belt, Major Osterkamp (centre) prepares to lead his *Gruppe* in its first ceremonial march-past through the unit's home town of Werl on 7 April 1936. Similarly attired to their *Kommandeur* are (left) Oberleutnant Walter Kienzle and (right) Leutnant Werner Mölders

Born in Düren, in the Rhineland, on 15 April 1892, Osterkamp – universally known as Theo – volunteered for the Imperial Navy's newly established *Marine-Fliegerkorps* within days of the outbreak of World War 1 in August 1914. After training, he was to spend nearly three years as an observer, before remustering as a pilot and joining I. *Marine-Feldjagdstaffel* (1st Naval Land-based Fighter Squadron) at Aertryke, in Flanders, on his 25th birthday.

Flying the Albatros D III, Leutnant *der Reserve* Osterkamp claimed his first aerial victory over Steenbrügge on 28 April 1917. A year later he was appointed leader of II. *Marine-Feldjagdstaffel*, and on 2 September 1918 – with his score standing at 27 – he was awarded the *Pour le Mérite*, or 'Blue Max'. Adding five more kills to his total in the final two months of the conflict, Osterkamp ended the war as Germany's highest scoring Naval Air Service fighter pilot.

There followed a brief stint as a member of the *Kampfgeschwader 'Sachsenberg'*, which was a volunteer unit set up to fight the Bolsheviks in Courland in 1919. However, by the beginning of 1920, like so many other ex-servicemen, Theo Osterkamp found himself demobilised and with a living to make as a civilian.

Despite forging a successful career as a car salesman, Osterkamp's first love remained flying. And when, in 1926, the offer of a job with the firm of Severa came along, he jumped at it. Operating floatplanes out of Kiel-Holtenau, and ostensibly formed to undertake civilian charter work, Severa also flew under contract for the German Navy, carrying out target-towing duties during fleet anti-aircraft gunnery exercises, artillery spotting and other ancillary tasks. From activities such as these, it was but a short step back into the military proper. And again Osterkamp needed little persuasion to make the change. He joined the still covert Luftwaffe on 1 August 1933 with the rank of hauptmann.

On the outbreak of World War 2, the now Oberstleutnant Osterkamp was commanding *Jagdfliegerschule* 1 at Werneuchen. Again in full rig, with the *Pour le Mérite* prominent at his throat, the benign and avuncular Osterkamp was by this time known throughout the Luftwaffe as 'Onkel Theo'

By the time war broke out in September 1939 Osterkamp had risen to the rank of oberstleutnant, and was commanding JFS 1 – the fighter pilot school at Werneuchen, northeast of Berlin. It was from here that he was ordered to Münster-Loddenheide to set up *Jagdgeschwader* 51.

Formally activated on 25 November 1939, the now Oberst Osterkamp's new unit thus became the third of the five *Jagdgeschwader* to

18 FLYING October 1, 1938

GERMAN-AUSTRIAN AIR FORCE

Following the annexation of Austria, Germany took over the military forces, including the small air force. This is now being brought up to the standard of German efficiency.

Modern German fighters on Askern Aerodrome, Vienna, the chief military airport in Austria.

The engine of a German-Austrian aeroplane being examined before a flight.

Fuelling a German training machine on the Askern Aerodrome.

Pretty work. German naval seaplanes flying a neat Vee formation.

The 1 October 1938 issue of *Flying* magazine devoted a page to the German annexation of Austria seven months earlier. The heading photograph is captioned, 'Modern German fighters on Askern (sic) Aerodrome, Vienna'. In fact, as their fuselage codes indicate, these are He 51s of 3./JG 135, which was . . .

be added to the Luftwaffe's order of battle during the eight months of the Phoney War. The *Stäbe* of JGs 27 and 77 had both been established on 1 October 1939, that of JG 1 followed on 8 December, and the last, *Stab* JG 54, came into being on 1 February 1940.

As yet, however, Oberst Osterkamp had only two component *Gruppen* to his organisational name, and even these were subordinated to other *Stäbe*. The first, currently based at Mannheim-Sandhofen under the control of JG 52, was Hauptmann Hans-Heinrich Brustellin's I./JG 51. This *Gruppe* could trace its history back nearly three years.

It was on 15 March 1937 that the then I./JG 135 had begun forming on He 51s. As the first *Jagdgruppe* to be activated within the area of *Luftkreis* (Air Region) V, which covered almost all of southern Germany, it took up residence on the still unfinished airfield at Bad Aibling, close to the Austrian border to the southeast of Munich.

Initially comprising just two *Staffeln*, I./JG 135, commanded by Major Max Ibel, was brought up to full establishment with the creation of a 3. *Staffel* under Oberleutnant Hans-Heinrich Brustellin on 1 July 1937. Towards the end of the year 3./JG 135's colourful Heinkel biplanes – each trimmed, appropriately enough, in the blue-and-white colours of Bavaria

... the *only* Staffel of I./JG 135 to have re-equipped with early model Bf 109s prior to the annexation. Here, the *Bertas* of 3. *Staffel* share the apron in front of the hangar of the Austrian Air Force's *Fliegerregiment* I with Do 17s of II./KG 155 on the day the Luftwaffe flew in to Aspern – 12 March 1938

– were replaced by Bf 109Bs wearing a more purposeful dark-green segmented camouflage finish. There were plans for the other two *Staffeln* to similarly re-equip early in 1938, but these were perforce put on hold by the *Führer's* decision to incorporate the land of his birth into the new Greater German Reich.

I./JG 135 was the only *Jagdgruppe* to be directly involved in Hitler's annexation of Austria on 12 March 1938 (although other units were to carry out 'demonstration flights' once the territories had been secured). From their base at Bad Aibling, hard by the Austrian border, Major Ibel's three *Staffeln* were each despatched to a different destination. Not surprisingly perhaps, it was 3./JG 135 – the only one equipped with Bf 109s – that was selected to cover the two *Gruppen* of Ju 52/3m transports flying the main body of German troops into Wien (Vienna)-Aspern airfield on the northeastern outskirts of the Austrian capital. Shortly afterwards, the He 51s of 1. and 2. *Staffeln* put down at Hörsching, near Linz, and Gross-Enzersdorf, east of Vienna, respectively.

Despite numerous post-war assertions to the contrary, in 1938 the vast majority of the Austrian population – general public and establishment alike - welcomed their German neighbours as ex-brothers in arms, rather than as occupying foreign troops. The small, but highly-trained, Austrian army and air force were quickly assimilated into the Wehrmacht, and the Heinkels of 1. and 2./JG 135, their presence no longer required, were soon recalled to Bad Aibling.

3./JG 135's Messerschmitts, however, were to remain in the *Ostmark* – or 'Eastern Marches', as Austria was renamed during its seven year existence as part of Hitler's Third Reich. On 14 March 1938, just 48 hours after touching down at Wien-Aspern, Oberleutnant Brustellin's

Staffel was redesignated as 1./JG 138 – the premier *Staffel* of a new Luftwaffe *Jagdgruppe* otherwise made up entirely of hitherto Austrian *Luftstreitkräfte* personnel (see *Osprey Aviation Elite Units 6 - Jagdgeschwader* 54 *'Grünherz'* for further details).

In exchange, an ex-Austrian *Staffel*, 5./*JaGeschw* II, commanded by Leutnant Erich Gerlitz and flying Fiat CR.32bis fighters, was transferred to Bad Aibling on 15 April to fill I./JG 135's now vacant third *Staffel* slot.

During the summer of 1938 all three of Ibel's *Staffeln* standardised on early Bf 109Ds. But further changes were afoot, for on 31 October Max Ibel departed to take over as *Kommodore* of JG 231 (later to become the wartime JG 3). He was replaced by Major Ernst *Freiherr* von Berg, whose arrival on 1 November 1938 coincided with the *Gruppe's* re-numbering as I./JG 233. The unit's new designation was brought about by the Luftwaffe's recent command restructuring from *Luftkreise* into *Luftwaffengruppenkommandos*. It indicated that the Bad Aibling *Gruppe* now formed part of the second *Jagdgeschwader* to be based in the area controlled by *Lw.Kdo* 3.

This cumbersome three-figure nomenclature was not to last long, however. On 1 May 1939 the introduction of a greatly simplified block designation system resulted in Major Berg's *Gruppe* emerging as I./JG 51, the premier *Jagdgruppe* of the new *Luftflotte* 3. At the same time the unit was busy converting from its original Bf 109Ds on to the latest E-models.

By now the war clouds were gathering ominously. In the summer of 1939, with Austria and Czechoslovakia already under his belt, Hitler's attention was focused firmly on Poland. Germany's *Führer* was not merely willing, but positively eager, to use force to subjugate his eastern neighbour. But he was uncertain how Britain and France would react if he attacked Poland. As a precaution, he ordered the strengthening of the aerial defences along the Reich's western borders.

Pictured at Mannheim-Sandhofen in the autumn of 1939, this pristine *Emil* of 3./JG 51 displays both the *Staffel's* (short-lived) 'Skeleton hand' emblem on the cowling and the new, more stylised 'Chamois on a mountain peak' I. *Gruppe* shield below the windscreen

The two pilots who scored I./JG 51's first aerial victories when they destroyed a French 'P-36' apiece near Weissenburg on 25 September 1939 – Oberleutnant Douglas Pitcairn (left), the *Kapitän* of 1. *Staffel*, and Unteroffizier Heinz Bär

Among the *Jagdgruppen* moved to the frontier with France was I./JG 51. On 26 August 1939 the unit departed Bad Aibling, its home base for the past two-and-a-half years, for Eutingen, southwest of Stuttgart, where it was subordinated to the *Stab* of JG 52 at nearby Böblingen. Six days later Hitler invaded Poland, and 48 hours after that, on 3 September 1939, Britain and France declared war on Germany.

I./JG 51 would spend the first two months of the Phoney War with its 40+ Bf 109Es divided between Eutingen and Speyer – the latter a field close to the Rhine south of Mannheim. It was during this period that the *Gruppe* gained its first three successes.

On 25 September elements of I./JG 51 were part of a mixed force of Bf 109s sent up to intercept a heavily escorted French reconnaissance Potez on its way to photograph German border defences around Bad Bergzabern, west of Karlsruhe. The enemy formations were spotted without difficulty, and shortly after midday six *Emils* of 1. *Staffel* succeeded in bouncing the reconnaissance machine's top cover, claiming the destruction of two Curtiss Hawk H-75As (which they identified as P-36s) near Weissenburg.

The first French fighter fell to the guns of Oberleutnant Douglas Pitcairn, who had taken over from Oberleutnant Hannes Trautloft as *Kapitän* of 1./JG 51 back in July 1938. The second was credited to one of

Pitcairn's more promising NCO pilots, Unteroffizier Heinz Bär (one of the *Jagdwaffe's* future 'greats', who would end the war flying Me 262 jets and with a final score of 221 confirmed victories).

Exactly three weeks later, on 16 October, Hauptmann Erich Gerlitz, *Staffelkapitän* of the ex-Austrian 3./JG 51, claimed a French Potez 63 south of Kaiserslautern. On the debit side, the *Gruppe* paid for these first three victories with the loss of a single 2. *Staffel* pilot who had been captured after forced landing behind French lines on 28 September.

Towards the end of October 1939 I./JG 51 was transferred to Mannheim-Sandhofen. Shortly after this move there was another change of command. On 31 October Major Ernst *Freiherr* von Berg was appointed *Kommandeur* of III./JG 26. His replacement was Hauptmann Hans-Heinrich Brustellin, erstwhile *Staffelkapitän* of the original Bf 109B-equipped 3./JG 135 at the time of the annexation of Austria.

The *Gruppe* would remain at Mannheim-Sandhofen under the control of JG 52 throughout the harsh winter of 1939-40. During this period its pilots accounted for four more French aircraft, but saw another two of their own number enter captivity after coming down over enemy territory. They also suffered their first two operational fatalities in take-off and emergency landing accidents.

In the meantime a second *Gruppe*, II./JG 51, had been brought into being. This unit was derived from one of the four individual *Jagdgruppen* that had been hurriedly set up in the final weeks prior to the outbreak of war. In the event, I./JG 71 consisted of only two *Staffeln*, commanded by Oberleutnants Heinz Schumann and Josef Fözö respectively.

Activated at Schleissheim on 15 July 1939 (around cadres provided by I./JG 51), 1. and 2./JG 71, both equipped with Bf 109Ds, transferred to Bad Aibling 11 days later. Here they spent a month working up alongside two reserve *Staffeln*, one likewise flying D-1s, the other operating ex-Czech Air Force Avia B 534 biplanes.

Bf 109D 'Red 6' of Oberleutnant Josef Fözö's 2./JG 71 is refuelled and re-armed shortly before the outbreak of war. The *Staffel's* 'weeping raven' emblem, seen here below the cockpit, would subsequently be moved to the aft fuselage, embellished with the exhortation *'Gott strafe England'*, and used as the badge of II./JG 51

On 26 August (the day I./JG 51 vacated Bad Aibling for Eutingen) the three Messerschmitt *Staffeln* were ordered to move to Fürstenfeldbruck to help bolster the aerial defences of Munich. Seventy-two hours later Oberleutnant Schumann's 1./JG 71 was detached and sent further north to Böblingen, near Stuttgart. These were the *Staffelns'* dispositions upon the outbreak of hostilities on 1 September. But on that same date came the parting of the ways when 1./JG 71 was redesignated 4./JG 52.

After two months at Fürstenfeldbruck, during which time they converted from Bf 109Ds to Es, the other two *Staffeln* transferred to Eutingen on 28 October. And it was here, on 1 November 1939, that II./JG 51 was formally activated.

A *Gruppenstab* was set up under Major Ernst-Günther Burggaller, who had been a member of the *'Richthofen' Geschwader* in World War 1. After making a name for himself as a highly successful motor racing driver in the inter-war years, he rejoined the Luftwaffe, where he had been serving latterly as the *Staffelkapitän* of 1./JG 2 'Richthofen'. Oberleutnant Josef Fözö's 2./JG 71 became 4./JG 51, while the hitherto *Reservestaffel*/JG 71 – led by Hauptmann Horst Tietzen, a veteran of the *Legion Condor* with seven victories to his credit – was redesignated as 5./JG 51.

A new 6. *Staffel* had to be created from scratch, with Oberleutnant Josef Priller, the NO (Communications Officer) of I./JG 51, being brought in from Mannheim-Sandhofen to assume command as its first *Kapitän*.

During the depths of the winter of 1939-40 II./JG 51 remained at Eutingen, with detachments being rotated to Friedrichshafen, on the shores of Lake Constance, where they enjoyed a welcome respite from the worst of the weather by being housed in one of the field's cavernous Zeppelin airship sheds. Throughout this period the *Gruppe* saw little or no operational activity. It claimed no successes and suffered just one casualty, Major Burggaller being killed when he struck the ground during a low-level flight west of Friedrichshafen on 2 February 1940.

A week later, under its new *Kommandeur*, Hauptmann Günther Matthes (previously the *Gruppen-Adjutant*), II./JG 51 was ordered to Böblingen. Until now the *Gruppe* had been subordinated directly to various regional commands. At Böblingen, which would be its base for the final three months of the Phoney War, II./JG 51 would come under the control of *Stab* JG 54, whose task was the defence of the southernmost (Upper Rhine) sector of Germany's border with France.

This period saw the opening of the *Gruppe's* scoreboard with three victories all within the space of one week. The first of these was a tethered observation balloon shot down in flames over the French bank of the Rhine to the southeast of Colmar by Oberleutnant Josef Fözö on 16 April.

This was not some kind of frivolous pastime as might at first appear. After nearly eight months of stalemate along the western front, such observation balloons played an important role in monitoring enemy activity. They were sited at strategically sensitive locations, and each was ringed by its own strong anti-aircraft defences. Consequently, the destruction of such a balloon was no easy matter, and rated at this time on a par with the downing of an enemy aircraft. Fözö's victim therefore took pride of place at the head of II./JG 51's score-sheet. It also enabled the *Kapitän* of 4. *Staffel* to shave off the luxurious beard he had been growing, and which he had sworn to keep until the *Gruppe* achieved its first victory!

Four days after the demise of the balloon, Hauptmann Horst Tietzen, *Staffelkapitän* of 5./JG 51, claimed his first victory of World War 2 to add to the seven he had scored in Spain. His adversary, a French Bloch MB 174 reconnaissance machine (misidentified as a Potez 63), went down some 30 miles inside German territory.

Twenty-four hours later, on 21 April 1940, the *Gruppe* caught another reconnaissance intruder well inside German airspace. This time it was a Spitfire PR IA of the RAF. A half-dozen *Emils* intercepted the Spitfire as it overflew their own Böblingen base, the Bf 109s overhauling their unsuspecting opponent from directly astern, using the enemy's contrail to hide their approach. When a burst of fire struck the Spitfire's engine, the pilot immediately reefed into a turn, hoping to get back to the safety of the French side of the Rhine. But it was not to be. After further attacks the engine finally gave out altogether, and Flg Off Cecil Milne was forced to bale out south of Stuttgart 'after first putting the machine into a steep dive to destroy its camera equipment'.

By this time Oberst Osterkamp's *Geschwaderstab* JG 51 had been declared operational. During the closing weeks of December 1939, two new commands had been set up to oversee all fighter activity along the western front. The two air fleets facing the western allies – *Luftflotte* 2 along the northern sector of the front and *Luftflotte* 3 in the south – had each established its own internal *Jagdfliegerführer* (literally 'Fighter-leader', more commonly abbreviated to *Jafü*) for the purpose.

On 1 January 1940 *Stab* JG 51 had been subordinated to *Jafü* 2, Generalmajor Kurt-Bertram von Döring, whose headquarters were situated at Dortmund, in the Ruhr. And on 12 February Osterkamp and his *Stab* were ordered forward from Münster to Bönninghardt, close to the Dutch border.

Bönninghardt also housed I./JG 26 and I./JG 20. But whereas the former would soon revert to the control of its parent *Geschwader*, and thus has only a passing role to play in the present narrative, I./JG 20 forms an

Emils of 1./JG 20 at rest on the grassy expanse of Brandenburg-Briest. The air of tranquility is deceptive. Hostilities have already been declared . . .

integral part of the history of JG 51 (it would be redesignated III./JG 51 after the successful conclusion of the forthcoming campaign against France).

I./JG 20 was another of the four *Jagdgruppen* that had been activated immediately prior to the outbreak of war. And, like I./JG 71, it too had consisted initially of only two *Staffeln*. Formed at Döberitz on 15 July 1939 from cadres drawn mainly from JG 2, the *Gruppe's* first *Kommandeur* was Major Siegfried Lehmann, who had previously headed the *Fliegerwaffenschule* (Air Weapons School) at Stolp-Reitz, in Pomerania. The *Kapitän* of Lehmann's 1. and 2./JG 20 were ex-*Legion Condor* veterans Oberleutnants Walter Oesau and Albrecht *Freiherr* von Minnigerode respectively, both of whom came from the *Stab* of I./JG 2.

On 26 August I./JG 20 was transferred from Döberitz to Strausberg, on the other (eastern) side of Berlin. Six days later, when Hitler invaded Poland, the *Gruppe* moved down to Sprottau, in Lower Silesia. Here, its 20+ Bf 109Es were tasked with protecting the area's many industrial targets from attack by the Polish Air Force. But the enemy's bombers never came. After an uneventful week, I./JG 20 was ordered back up to Brandenburg-Briest on 9 September.

During the two months the *Gruppe* was to remain at Brandenburg-Briest, near Berlin, it experienced both a change of command and an increase in size to a full three-*Staffel* establishment. On 18 September Major Lehmann returned to Stolp-Reitz to become *Kommandeur* of the *Jagdfliegerschule* (Fighter Pilot School) newly established there. His replacement at the head of I./JG 20 was Hauptmann Hannes Trautloft, ex-*Staffelkapitän* of 2./JG 77. And on 1 November a 3. *Staffel* was set up under Oberleutnant Richard Kraut.

3./JG 20 had, in fact, been activated at Döberitz, and the rest of the *Gruppe* joined it there from Briest six days later. Up until this time, I./JG 20 had been operating under the control of *Stab* JG 2. For the next three winter months spent at Döberitz it would be subordinated to *Stab*

. . . and the pilot of 'White 3' is settling himself into the cockpit for another defensive patrol of the Greater Berlin area. This close-up shows to advantage the *Staffel's* 'bow and arrow' emblem, as well as the machine's two-tone dark green/black green splinter finish

The second of I./JG 20's two original *Staffeln* opted for a black cat as their unit badge. Whether the feline carefully picking its way along the top of the cowling was the original model is not known, but it certainly displays a remarkable likeness!

JG 3, but its responsibilities remained the same – the aerial defence of the German capital.

On 15 February 1940 Oberleutnant Richard Kraut was appointed *Gruppenkommandeur* of I./JG 76. The officer selected to be the new *Kapitän* of 3./JG 20 was the *Staffel's* senior pilot, Oberleutnant Arnold Lignitz. And just under a week later, on 21 February, I./JG 20 was transferred westwards from Döberitz to Bönninghardt to join I./JG 26 as the second *Gruppe* to come under the command of Oberst Theo Osterkamp's burgeoning JG 51.

When I./JG 20 moved up to Bönninghardt, close to the Dutch border, early in 1940, its machines were given a coat of *hellblau* paint and a new *Gruppe* badge, 'The Axe of the Lower Rhine', denoting both its role and geographical location. The first enemy aircraft to feel the weight of I./JG 20's axe was a Photographic Development Unit Spitfire of the RAF

I./JG 51's *Emils* were also sporting *hellblau* camouflage finish (plus correctly proportioned and positioned national insignia) as the Phoney War dragged to a close. The sense of expectancy here at Krefeld in April 1940 is almost palpable

It was during the last 11 weeks of the Phoney War, while stationed at Bönninghardt under *Stab* JG 51, that I./JG 20 finally opened its score-sheet. The *Gruppe's* first victim was another RAF reconnaissance Spitfire, albeit pre-dating II./JG 51's destruction of the No 212 Sqn machine described earlier by almost a month. Unlike the latter, however, the pilot of the Photographic Development Unit Spitfire intercepted by 1./JG 20's Leutnant Harald Jung over Kleve on 22 March 1940 did not survive the encounter. Although he too baled out, Plt Off Wheatley's parachute failed to open. His aircraft crashed in marshy ground bordering the River Waal near the Dutch border town of Nijmegen.

The following month, on 14 April, Oberleutnant Arnold Lignitz, *Staffelkapitän* of 3./JG 20, caught an RAF Blenheim carrying out a reconnaissance of the same general area to the northeast of Kleve. Intercepted over Emmerich, the No 57 Sqn bomber was also last seen going down in flames just beyond the Dutch border.

By this time a third *Gruppe* had been added to Oberst Osterkamp's *Stab* JG 51. On 22 March 1940 Hauptmann Hans-Heinrich Brustellin's I./JG 51 had been transferred from Mannheim-Sandhofen to Krefeld, some 25 km to the south of Bönninghardt. Almost four months to the day since setting up his *Geschwaderstab* JG 51, Theo Osterkamp at last had one of his 'own' *Gruppen* under his direct command!

A fourth and final *Gruppe* was assigned to *Stab* JG 51 the following month when, on 20 April, Hauptmann Werner Andres' II./JG 27 flew in to Bönninghardt to join I./JG 26 and I./JG 20.

Not one of Osterkamp's four component *Gruppen* managed to down an enemy aircraft during the Phoney War's final days. But it would not be long before they found themselves in the middle of a real shooting war.

THE BATTLES OF FRANCE AND BRITAIN

As part of *Jafü* 2 on the northern flank of the western front, the initial task of Oberst Osterkamp's *Stab* JG 51, and its four attached *Gruppen*, was to support the air landings in Holland and Belgium. Once these had been accomplished, Osterkamp's fighters would cover the ground force's subsequent advance across the Low Countries and into France.

What none of the pilots knew was that their operations were part of a gigantic bluff designed to lure British and French troops forward into Belgium, thus leaving a dangerous gap behind them through which the main German assault would be launched out of the Ardennes hills to the south, across the open plains of Picardy and to the Channel coast.

The strategic planning for the *Blitzkrieg* in the west was a model of its kind. Complete surprise was achieved, the enemy were wrong-footed and thrown on to the defensive from the start, and nearly every objective was attained. At a lower level, however, it was a different story. The Luftwaffe – and its fighters in particular – were far from as strong and well organised as the pre-war world had been led to believe.

Even after eight months of hostilities, few *Jagdgeschwader* were at full complement, with their three component *Gruppen* operating together as a whole. During the seven weeks of the campaign in the west, it was the norm, rather than the exception, for a fighter *Stab* to be controlling a miscellany of *Gruppen* from other *Jagdgeschwader* whose numbers waxed and waned according to immediate operational demands.

Stab JG 51 provides a striking – perhaps the extreme – example. During the *Blitzkrieg* against the Low Countries and France, Osterkamp controlled, at one stage or another, a total of no fewer than ten(!) different *Jagdgruppen*. The lengths of time each remained under his command ranged from a single day to – in one instance only – the full seven weeks that the campaign lasted.

It would be both complicated and confusing to chart the activities of all ten of these *Jagdgruppen* during this period. Space dictates that attention be focussed solely on those *Gruppen* relating directly to JG 51.

'Fall Gelb' ('Case Yellow') – the *Blitzkrieg* in the west – was launched before first light on the morning of 10 May 1940. Oberst Osterkamp himself flew at the head of his three Bönninghardt-based *Gruppen* as they began taking off at 0520 hrs to attack three Dutch airfields. Their orders were to destroy the enemy aircraft on the ground before the arrival of German airborne forces. They were then to return to Bönninghardt to refuel and re-arm, before scrambling again at 0740 hrs, this time to provide a fighter umbrella above the paratroops' dropping zones.

After rendezvousing over Wesel at 3000 metres, Osterkamp led Hauptmann Hannes Trautloft's I./JG 20 to their assigned target – the airfield at Eindhoven. Flying in a wide arc around the objective, Osterkamp planned to attack the field from the west. By approaching from this unexpected direction, with the last of the darkness in the sky at his back, Osterkamp hoped to achieve the element of surprise. He need not have bothered, for in his own words, 'Down to 1000 metres for the final run-in, descending to little more than 20 metres, no defensive fire. Line the right-hand hangar up in my gunsight, thumb on the trigger – the hangar doors are standing wide open, not an aircraft in sight – empty, empty, nothing at all!'

The *Kommodore* immediately called off the attack over the R/T, ordering instead that his pilots seek other military targets of opportunity in the area before returning to base. By the time they took off again for the second of the morning's missions, the first wave of paratroops had already landed, their abandoned parachutes 'dotting the fields and meadows around Rotterdam like a crop of huge white mushrooms'.

Next to come in were another three large groups of Ju 52/3m transports carrying yet more airborne forces and their equipment. Osterkamp's pilots escorted them in to their assigned landing zones around Rotterdam and The Hague. Many of the Junkers even put down on the excellent Dutch roads that ran straight and wide between these two points. Encountering no aerial opposition, the German fighters carried out strafing runs to suppress the enemy's anti-aircraft defences.

By the end of the first day of the *Blitzkrieg* in the west, although the attached I./JG 26 and II./JG 27 had been credited with eight victories between them, neither Theo Osterkamp's *Stab* JG 51 nor Hannes Trautloft's I./JG 20 had been able to claim a single aerial kill. Worse still, the latter suffered the day's only fatality when Feldwebel Walter Hoppe of 1./JG 20 crashed close to the Rhine from causes unknown.

11 May 1940 was very much a repetition of the opening day. Despite further incursions in force into Dutch airspace, success continued to elude *Stab* JG 51 and I./JG 20. And Hauptmann Trautloft's *Gruppe* lost another pilot. This time it was Oberleutnant Albrecht *Freiherr* von Minnigerode, the *Kapitän* of his 2. *Staffel*, whose *Emil* was brought down by Dutch anti-aircraft fire near Tiel.

Unlike most of the Luftwaffe pilots and aircrew who were shot down over French territory during the coming days and weeks of the campaign in the west – the majority of whom would be returned to Germany after the French surrender – 'Minni' was quickly taken to England and subsequently sat out the rest of the war as a PoW in Canada.

It was not until 12 May that *Stab* JG 51 and I./JG 20 claimed a success apiece. The latter's French Potez 63 was credited to 3 *Staffel's* Leutnant Hans Kolbow. *Stab* JG 51's opening kill (a Fokker G-I) was downed by the *Kommodore* himself, this beingTheo Osterkamp's first victory since the last of his 32 World War 1 victims went down more than 21 years earlier!

Oberst Osterkamp's other *Gruppe*, I./JG 51, based at Krefeld, had also been supporting airborne operations over Holland during these first three days of the campaign in the west. It was a task they carried out with considerable success, claiming four victories without loss to themselves on 10 May. Three of their four victims had been Dutch Fokker D XXI fighters, among them a first for future *Experte* and Knight's Cross winner Oberleutnant Richard Leppla, *Kapitän* of 3. *Staffel*.

The following day I./JG 51 was credited with the destruction of five RAF Hurricanes (all from No 17 Sqn) in a brief but bitter late afternoon melée near Rotterdam. Two pilots, Leutnant Ernst Terry of the *Gruppenstab* and 3. *Staffel's* Oberleutnant Heinrich Krafft, opened their scores with a pair each. But this time there was a price to pay.

Unteroffizier Fritz Schreiter, who had in fact claimed the first of the five Hurricanes to go down, was himself hit moments later. He baled out over Waalhaven airfield and spent the next four days in Dutch captivity. Fellow 3. *Staffel* member Unteroffizier Franz Schild was less fortunate. Shot down south of Rotterdam, his was the sad distinction of being the first of the very nearly 500 pilots of JG 51 to be reported killed or missing in action before war's end.

For the immediate future, however, I./JG 51 was to be separated again from its parent *Geschwader*. On 13 May Hauptmann Brustellin led his *Gruppe* down to Dünstekoven, a landing ground on the west bank of the Rhine near Bonn. Here, they came under the command of JG 27. This unit formed the fighter component of Generalmajor von Richthofen's VIII. *Fliegerkorps*, whose Stuka dive-bombers would be spearheading the main German armoured thrust out of the Eifel/Ardennes hills to the Channel coast.

For the remainder of the month I./JG 51 was kept busy flying a gruelling succession of Stuka escort and *freie Jagd* missions as they helped clear the skies above the Panzers of Army Group A racing for the French Channel ports. During this period the *Gruppe* added a further 25 enemy aircraft to its collective scoreboard. Its most successful day was 21 May. This opened with an early morning clash over Abbeville which netted five French Morane MS 406 fighters. It closed with a brace of RAF Hurricanes brought down near Samer by Douglas Pitcairn and Heinz Bär, the duo who had opened the *Gruppe's* scoring with a 'Curtiss P-36' apiece back in September 1939.

It was not only the pilots who were being pushed to the limit. In order to keep up with the rampaging Panzers, ground staff had to move base three times in the space of a week. On 16 May they departed Dünstekoven for Neufchâteau, in Belgium. Four days later they crossed the border into France, where they set up camp at Guise, southeast of Cambrai, for all of three days, before transferring yet further forward to Tupigny. It was at Guise, on 22 May, that I./JG 51 suffered its second, and last fatality, of the *Blitzkrieg* in the west when a Bf 109 landing back after a mission rammed a Ju 87 of III./StG 2 taxiing out to take off.

Meanwhile, still in the north, *Stab* JG 51 and I./JG 20 continued to support Army Group B's push through the Low Countries. I./JG 20's sole success of 13 May – a French Hawk H-75A downed over Halsteren – is noteworthy for providing the first wartime victory (after the eight achieved in Spain with *Legion Condor*) for another of the Luftwaffe's future *Experten*, Oberleutnant Walter Oesau.

On 16 May, the day after the Dutch capitulation, Osterkamp's *Stab* and I./JG 20 also moved forward into occupied territory, leaving Bönninghardt for the 70 km hop across the border to Eindhoven, in Holland. Within 24 hours of its arrival, I./JG 20 found itself engaged in a brief, but bloody, confrontation with French Hawk H-75As over the island of Walcheren, in the Scheldt Estuary. Five of the enemy fighters

Future 'centurion' Oberleutnant Walter Oesau, seen here in the fur-collared flying jacket deep in conversation with 'black men' (i.e. groundcrew) of his 1./JG 20, scored his first kill of World War 2 on 13 May 1940. Note the 'bow and arrow' emblem now in black on the *hellblau* cowling of the *Staffel's* Bf 109s

were claimed in as many minutes, but the *Gruppe* lost two of its own NCO pilots – one shot down and killed over the centre of the island, and the other captured after forced landing through lack of fuel.

The days that followed saw a marked reduction in aerial activity on the northern flank of the German offensive as the Allies threw almost everything they had left into a final attempt to stave off the catastrophe looming to the south. On 20 May I./JG 20 transferred to Woensdrecht. This was its base for the next eight days, as the unit patrolled the Belgium and French coastlines from Zeebrugge to Calais without tangible result.

The move to Ghent-St Denis on 29 May brought about an immediate change. The evacuation of British troops from Dunkirk – less than 100 km away – was by now in its fourth day. On the evening of their arrival at Ghent, I./JG 20 claimed three RAF fighters over the Dunkirk region – a Spitfire each for *Gruppenkommandeur* Hauptmann Hannes Trautloft and Leutnants Hans Kolbow and Karl-Heinz Schnell of 3. *Staffel.*

Forty-eight hours later on 31 May, as the evacuation of the BEF was reaching its peak, a series of bomber escort and *freie Jagd* missions over the beaches and inshore shipping lanes resulted in the *Gruppe's* highest-scoring day to date with no fewer than a dozen enemy aircraft destroyed.

The first was a solitary Lysander shot down off Ostende during an early afternoon sortie. As evening approached, another sweep to the north and west of Dunkirk produced five confirmed kills (all Spitfires), including a second for Hannes Trautloft and a pair for Walter Oesau. A last patrol of the same areas in mid-evening brought claims for six more victories. Three of these were submitted by Oberleutnant Arnold Lignitz, *Kapitän* of 3. *Staffel* – a brace of Spitfires ten minutes apart, and the day's last, like the first, a Lysander.

The casualties had not been all one-sided, however. 31 May had cost I./JG 20 two pilots killed, while Leutnant Hans Kolbow, having sent a Fleet Air Arm Skua into the sea off Nieuport, was himself hit by return fire

'Onkel Theo' (right) awards the Iron Cross, First Class, to Hauptmann Horst Tietzen, *Staffelkapitän* of 5./JG 51. In the background II. *Gruppe's Kommandeur*, Hauptmann Günther Matthes, looks on approvingly – or should that be impassively?

as he next tried to tackle a formation of No 264 Sqn Defiants. He wrote off his fighter in a belly landing south of Calais.

In operational terms, the following day was something of an anti-climax. A brief clash between 1./JG 20 and a flight of Blenheims off Ostende ended with a fourth victory for *Staffelkapitän* Oberleutnant Walter Oesau and the wounding of one of his pilots.

That 1 June 1940 was, however, to be an important and significant date in the history of JG 51. For this was the day that Oberst Osterkamp's *Stab* joined I./JG 20 at Ghent-St Denis (after a week spent at Antwerp-Deurne). At the same time, I./JG 51's temporary attachment to JG 27 came to an end and Hauptmann Brustellin's *Gruppe* was returned to Osterkamp's control. And it was on this date too that II./JG 51 was released by *Luftflotte* 3 – the command to which it had been subordinated since its activation on 1 November 1939, latterly as part of JG 54 – and transferred up to *Luftflotte* 2, there also finally to join its parent *Stab*.

Compared to their northern brethren, Hauptmann Günther Matthes' II./JG 51 in the far south had spent a very uneventful first fortnight of the *Blitzkrieg* patrolling the upper reaches of the Rhine and the skies of Alsace beyond. The *Gruppe's* sole success during this period had been a French Mureaux 117 reconnaissance aircraft downed northwest of Strasbourg on 12 May. It did not claim their next victory, a Potez 63, until 26 May.

This was the day the unit received orders to begin moving forward. 6. *Staffel* was the first to leave German soil, departing Böblingen for Dinant, in southern Belgium. The rest of the *Gruppe* took off 48 hours later for Emptinne, by which time 6./JG 51 was already in action over Dunkirk. The four-minute melée off the evacuation beaches shortly after midday on 28 May had sufficed not only to open 6. *Staffel's* score-sheet, two of the four RAF fighters downed also provided firsts for yet two more future Knight's Cross recipients in Oberleutnant Josef Priller and Leutnant Herbert Huppertz.

II./JG 51's arrival at Vitry-en-Artois on 1 June meant that, for the first time ever, Oberst Theo Osterkamp had command of what was, in effect, his complete *Geschwader* (I./JG 20 had long been regarded as his rightful III. *Gruppe* in all but name).

But the proud *Kommodore* was not allowed to enjoy this unaccustomed state of affairs for long. *'Fall Gelb'*, the first phase of the conquest of France, was drawing to a close. The last Allied troops were being lifted off the beaches of Dunkirk. 1./JG 20's Walter Oesau claimed a Blenheim in the area on 1 June, and Josef Priller and Unteroffizier Arthur Haase of 6./JG 51 were each credited with a fighter southwest of the town 24 hours later. Now *'Fall Rot'* ('Case Red') – the assault on the main bulk of the French army – was about to be launched.

'Rot' was preceded by large-scale bombing raids on targets in the greater Paris area on 3 June in which both *Stab* JG 51 and I./JG 20 were involved. Thereafter, although records are contradictory, it appears that I./JG 51 was reassigned to JG 27 – at least briefly – to take part in the major thrust southwards into the heart of France. On 5 June the *Gruppe* downed four Allied aircraft, including a first (identified as a Blenheim) for *Kommandeur* Hauptmann Hans-Heinrich Brustellin, north of the French capital. The following day it claimed four LeO 451 bombers attacking a German bridgehead across the Somme canal.

Then, on 10 June, I./JG 51 was suddenly withdrawn from France altogether and transferred to Jever, in Germany, to come under the command of *Stab* JG 1, defending the North Sea coastline. From here, 11 days later, it was sent to Leeuwarden, in Holland. On the afternoon of the unit's arrival, its pilots were credited with a trio of twin-engined bombers north of the Dutch island of Texel. Identified at the time as 'de Havillands', these were more likely to have been Hudsons of RAF Coastal Command.

Meanwhile, Osterkamp's *Stab* JG 51, together with II./JG 51 and I./JG 20 (plus a third *Gruppe* to make up for Hauptmann Brustellin's absent I./JG 51), had been operating on the extreme right-hand flank of the renewed German offensive, supporting the push westwards along the French Channel coast towards Brittany. II./JG 51 and I./JG 20 saw relatively little aerial action during *'Fall Rot'*. By the time of the French armistice they had added just five and six more victories respectively to their collective totals. One of the four Blenheims claimed by II./JG 51 over Abbeville on 8 June had provided another first for *Gruppenkommandeur* Hauptmann Günther Matthes (two of the others fell to Josef Priller).

The defeat of France would leave just one enemy remaining – Great Britain. The next logical step for the seemingly invincible *Wehrmacht* would be a cross-Channel invasion of southern England. Theo Osterkamp, as well aware of this fact as anybody, was unhappy that his *Gruppen* were being directed westwards towards Normandy and the Cotentin peninsula, far beyond effective range of the British coast for his short-legged Bf 109s. The scene of any future action, he knew, would have to centre on the Pas de Calais – the very area over which he had operated

Illustrating the conditions under which Osterkamp's units operated during the rapid advance through France, this *Emil* of the *Gruppenstab* I./JG 20 is refuelled in a particularly lush meadow. The machine's 'Chevron circle' markings identify it as the mount of the *Gruppe* TO, Leutnant Werner Pichon-Kalau vom Hofe. After claiming just three kills – a trio of Defiants in the action of 19 July 1940 – Pichon-Kalau vom Hofe would accompany *Kommandeur* Hannes Trautloft to JG 54

against the 'lords' (the term he always used to describe the British) during World War 1.

In his own account of this period, Osterkamp confesses to resorting to a piece of behind the scenes string-pulling. Whether true or not, it is on record that on 22 June – the day the Armistice was signed at Compiègne – JG 51 had been ordered to about face and transfer up into the Pas de Calais, the *Stab* going to Le Touquet, II./JG 51 to Desvres and I./JG 20 to St Omer-Wizernes.

Thus, unlike most Luftwaffe units, who were given a well-deserved break after the rigours of the French campaign – including some who were even rotated back to the Reich for rest and re-equipment – JG 51 transitioned almost seamlessly from Battle of France into Battle of Britain. In fact, so keen was Theo Osterkamp to get to grips with the RAF that he even found an excuse not to take part in the victory fly-past over Paris – this tiresome chore he left to his senior *Gruppenkommandeur*.

The *Kommodore's* determination soon paid off. On 25 June, just 72 hours after taking up residence at Desvres, 6./JG 51's Oberleutnant Josef Priller claimed a Spitfire near Boulogne. Before the month was out, II./JG 51 had accounted for four more RAF machines over the Pas de Calais and Straits of Dover. In the same period I./JG 20 were credited with eight victories – seven of them on 30 June alone, when it downed four Blenheims attacking the airfield at Merville, as well as a trio of Spitfires.

Slowly, almost leisurely, Luftwaffe Commander-in-Chief Hermann Göring began to assemble his forces for the forthcoming battle. The first prerequisite for any invasion attempt would be to establish air superiority over the Channel and close it to British shipping. It was not deemed necessary to employ the whole weight of an entire *Fliegerkorps* to clear the Straits of Dover. Instead, a mixed battle group of Dornier bombers, Ju 87 Stuka dive-bombers and Bf 110 *Zerstörer* was set up. As the only *Jagdgeschwader* yet deployed on the Channel coast, Osterkamp's JG 51 was charged with providing the fighter protection for this motley force.

The savvy Theo Osterkamp chose to interpret his orders to 'protect' the bombers with a certain amount of licence. Rather than restrict his pilots to close escort of the Do 17s and Ju 88s (the very tactic that a furious Göring would wrongly impose upon his fighters later in the Battle), Osterkamp initiated a series of free-ranging *freie Jagd* sweeps along the Kent coast aimed at challenging RAF Fighter Command's defences.

This deliberate provocation inevitably led to clashes. It also heralded a new chapter in the history of JG 51. Personal and unit scores began to climb dramatically, with the individual victories of the recent French campaign giving way to multiple daily scores, often running into double figures as the Battle intensified. But, faced for the first time with a determined and well organised enemy (and one, moreover, who enjoyed the incalculable advantage of radar ground control – a fact unknown at the time to the Germans), JG 51's losses would also begin to rise.

The first RAF victims of Osterkamp's one-man 'lean into England' were a brace of Hurricanes claimed by II./JG 51 near Dover on 4 July. It was on this date that Hauptmann Hannes Trautloft's I./JG 20 officially became part of the *Geschwader* upon being redesignated III./JG 51 – an event duly marked three days later when Oberleutnant Walter Oesau and three pilots of his new 7./JG 51 were credited with a Spitfire each off Dover.

Inevitably, though, a price was going to have to be paid for these incursions. And it was Oesau's 7. *Staffel* that suffered JG 51's first fatality of the Battle the following day when Unteroffizier Konrad Schneiderberger was shot down during another foray over the Straits.

II./JG 51 was also in action on this same 8 July, and in a separate incident, a *Schwarm* (four aircraft) of Oberleutnant Josef Fözö's 4. *Staffel* was headed off and chased inland by Spitfires. Leutnant Johann Böhm's "White 4" was hit in the radiator and he was forced to make a spectacular wheels-up landing in a field of ewes on the slopes of Bladbean Hill above the village of Elham, in Kent. The first Luftwaffe fighter to be shot down over Britain, Böhm's broken-backed *Emil*, with its strange 'weeping raven' device on the rear fuselage, was a source of huge interest to both locals and officialdom alike!

II. *Gruppe* also sustained JG 51's next two losses when 5. *Staffel* had a pilot killed in a dogfight on each of the two succeeding days. The latter date (10 July) is now recognised by most British historians as the start of the Battle proper. It gave rise to a series of violent clashes over a Channel convoy westbound through the Straits of Dover. By day's end, III./JG 51 had been credited with no fewer than ten Spitfires – including three more for Walter Oesau – against two of its own Bf 109s crash-landed back in France (one of which was written off).

On 12 July, its temporary detachment to JG 1 and its defence of the Dutch coast at an end, Hauptmann Hans-Heinrich Brustellin's I./JG 51 arrived at Pihen, in the Pas de Calais – not far from the *Stab's* new base at Cap Blanc Nez. For the second time in JG 51's short history, *Kommodore* Oberst Osterkamp had all three of the *Geschwader's* component *Gruppen* under his direct command. As if to celebrate the fact, Osterkamp claimed a Spitfire over Dover exactly 24 hours later. Whether this was his sixth or second victory of World War 2 is open to debate. What is not in question is that it was to be his last. In just ten days' time he would have to relinquish command of the *Geschwader* he had created.

The one major event of Oberst Osterkamp's last week as *Kommodore* was III./JG 51's virtual annihilation of an entire RAF fighter squadron on 19 July. Newly flown down from Scotland, the crews of the two-seater

A close-up of the II./JG 51 *Gruppe* badge adorning Johann Böhm's 'White 4'. This raven had good reason to weep – not only was his the first Bf 109 to be brought down over England (on 8 July 1940), note how close that bullet hole came to clipping his beak!

Defiants of No 141 Sqn were relatively inexperienced, and stood little chance when ordered to patrol a line south of Folkestone shortly after midday on that date.

The only thing that the anachronistic Defiant had going for it – the element of surprise at encountering a single-engined fighter with no forward armament whatsoever, but encumbered instead with an unwieldy four-gun dorsal turret – had been exploited (but at the same time cruelly exposed) by No 141 Sqn's sister unit No 264 Sqn over Dunkirk six weeks earlier.

Hauptmann Trautloft's pilots were thus fully aware of their opponents' fatal shortcomings. A concerted attack from below and astern – the Defiant's most vulnerable blind spot – resulted in claims for 11 aircraft destroyed in just eight minutes! The first had fallen to Hannes Trautloft, while that credited to Walter Oesau took the latter's score to ten, making him the first member of JG 51 to reach double figures.

Although the above claims are exaggerated, indicative perhaps of the ferocity and confusion of the assault on the unsuspecting two-seaters, the true outcome of the encounter was bad enough – four Defiants sent spiralling into the Channel in less than 60 seconds, a fifth crashing on Dover, and two others forced landing (one a write-off, and the other damaged but repairable). The cost to Trautloft had been a single Bf 109 damaged by return fire, which crash-landed back in France, although a 9. *Staffel* pilot was killed in a subsequent clash with other RAF fighters.

It was on 23 July that Oberst Theo Osterkamp was finally forced to relinquish command of JG 51. His removal from office had nothing to do with the cull of ageing *Kommodores* instigated by an irate *Reichsmarschall* Göring later in the Battle to counteract what he then perceived to be a 'lack of aggression' among his *Jagdgeschwader*. In fact, Osterkamp's success was his own undoing. His operational experience and leadership skills made him the ideal candidate to become the next *Jafü* 2 – the fighter leader responsible for controlling all fighter units now stationed in the Pas de Calais, and surrounding areas.

The cheery and avuncular Osterkamp would be a hard act to follow. But there was one man, although entirely different in character, who was

I. *Gruppe's* first fatality of the Battle of Britain was 1. *Staffel's* Oberfeldwebel Oskar Sicking. A victim of one of the early Channel convoy engagements, Sicking was killed while attempting to bale out over the French coast on 20 July. His aircraft crashed on the beach near Audighem at low tide and burned out

Although the new *Kommodore's* baptism of fire over the Channel was not altogether auspicious, Major Werner Mölders soon stamped his own paternal air of authority on the *Geschwader*

ideally suited to take his place. Already something of a national hero, the 27-year-old Major Werner Mölders had been the highest scoring member of the *Legion Condor*, returning from Spain with 14 victories to his credit. More recently, as *Gruppenkommandeur* of III./JG 53 during the Battle of France, he had been the first to achieve 20 kills against the Western Allies, for which he became the first fighter pilot to be awarded the prestigious Knight's Cross.

But Mölders's formal assumption of command of JG 51 on 27 July was not to be without incident. He had not flown operationally since being shot down on the opening day of *'Fall Rot'* and languishing for more than two weeks in French captivity. The outgoing *Kommodore* tried to impart a few well-meaning words of advice on the different type of war now being imposed upon the Luftwaffe by the 'lords' across the Channel.

His warnings went unheeded. Werner Mölders elected to lead elements of his I. and II. *Gruppen* on a bomber-escort mission to Dover the very next day. Intercepted by Spitfires when halfway across the Straits, the bombers turned away as JG 51's fighters attempted to cover their withdrawal. Major Mölders was credited with a Spitfire over Dover (victory 26), and two pilots of I. *Gruppe* made similar claims. But 2. *Staffel's* Gefreiter Martin Gebhardt was shot into the Channel and killed. And only the prompt intervention of Oberleutnant Richard Leppla, *Staffelkapitän* of 3./JG 51, saved his new *Kommodore* from possibly sharing the same fate.

Leppla chased a Spitfire off the tail of an already wounded Mölders as he nursed his badly damaged machine back towards the French coast. The

Kommodore survived the subsequent belly-landing without further serious injury, but was nonetheless forced – upon the express orders of the *Reichsmarschall* himself – to spend the next ten days under supervision in a Berlin hospital. Theo Osterkamp welcomed the unexpected opportunity to return to 'his' JG 51 as acting *Kommodore* in the interim. During this period the *Geschwader* claimed a further 20 Spitfires (and a solitary 'Curtiss') – all of them over the Straits or in the Dover area – for three of its pilots killed and one wounded.

But the first phase of the Battle was drawing to a close. Operations to deny the narrows to British shipping, in which JG 51 had played such a major part, had been largely successful. Now it was time to take the war inland and, in true *Blitzkrieg* style, attempt to destroy the enemy's air force on the ground. Hitler's War Directive No 17, dated 1 August 1940, read in part, 'The Luftwaffe is to overpower the English Air Force with all the strength at its command and in the shortest possible time. The attacks are to be directed primarily against flying units, their ground installations, and their supply organisations'.

Werner Mölders' return from Berlin on 7 August, sporting a special pilot's badge in gold and diamonds awarded by a grateful *Führer*, coincided with the intensification of the battle against the RAF. JG 51 was now but one of five *Jagdgeschwader* stationed in and around the Pas de Calais. The days of the freebooting Osterkamp were over. The Straits of Dover were no longer JG 51's own private domain. The *Geschwader* had become just one part of the powerful Luftwaffe armada assembled along the Channel coast ready to deliver the *coup de grâce* to RAF Fighter Command forces in southern England.

After several postponements, the massed attack on RAF airfields and other targets in southern England was finally scheduled for 13 August. But *'Adlertag'* ('Eagle Day') misfired badly. A combination of adverse weather conditions and a breakdown in communications played havoc with the Luftwaffe's well-laid plans. Some bombers arrived over England devoid of their promised fighter cover, while elsewhere other *Jagdgruppen* circled aimlessly in mid-Channel awaiting rendezvous with bombers that never appeared. JG 51's role in *'Adlertag'* could hardly be termed pivotal. By day's end its pilots had put in a claim for a single Spitfire (unconfirmed) and had had one pilot wounded off Cap Gris Nez.

It was a different story 48 hours later when the Luftwaffe mounted another all-out effort – its greatest of the entire Battle of Britain, in fact – again targeted mainly at airfields. All three of Werner Mölders' *Gruppen* were involved, claiming no fewer than 19 RAF fighters between them.

I./JG 51's six victories included a pair each for Oberleutnant Hermann-Friedrich Joppien and Hauptmann Ernst Wiggers, the *Kapitäne* of 1. and 2. *Staffeln*. The second of Joppien's two Hurricanes

Luftwaffe Commander-in-Chief *Reichsmarschall* Hermann Göring pays a visit of inspection to the Channel front. And judging from the expressions here, all is clearly not well. These officers are, from left to right, Göring, General Gustav Kastner-Kirdorf of the RLM, General Bruno Loerzer, GOC II. *Fliegerkorps*, and Werner Mölders (note the latter's gold and diamond pilot's badge below the Iron Cross on his breast pocket)

Individually, many pilots went from strength to strength during the Battle of Britain. Amongst the most successful was Josef Föző, seen here vividly describing one of his 14 Channel front victories to his groundcrew. Leutnant Erich Hohagen (right), who was to claim 11 kills during the same period, also listens attentively

took his total to ten. Another Hurricane had fallen to *Gruppenkommandeur* Hauptmann Hans-Heinrich Brustellin, but he was himself seriously wounded in the encounter. Brustellin nonetheless managed to get back to Pihen, where he crash-landed. Fortunately, he was hauled out of the twisted wreckage of his *Emil* before it was completely gutted by fire. Brustellin was off operations for the next seven weeks, during which time the *Gruppe* was ably led in his absence by acting *Kommandeur* Oberleutnant Richard Leppla, *Kapitän* of 3. *Staffel.*

II./JG 51 had an even more successful 15 August with ten victories (all Hurricanes – no sign of 'Spitfire snobbery' here!) to show for its three separate missions of the day over Kent and Essex. All three *Staffelkapitäne* were among the claimants, 5./JG 51's Hauptmann Horst Tietzen downing a trio, while Oberleutnants Josef Föző and Josef Priller of 4. and 6. *Staffeln* got a single kill each.

Twenty-four hours later, on 16 August, the *Gruppe* went two better. Its 12 claims on this date made it the unit's highest scoring day of the Battle of Britain. It had cost II./JG 51 one pilot, who had baled out after a skirmish with Spitfires over Faversham. Then came 18 August, and what one eminent historian has been moved to describe as 'The Hardest Day'.

Once again all three *Gruppen* of JG 51 were involved, but this time not only did Hauptmann Günther Matthes' II. *Gruppe* come a poor third in

5./JG 51's *Staffelkapitän* Horst Tietzen is given help donning his life-jacket . . .

the scoring stakes – with claims for just two Hurricanes – it also suffered the *Geschwader's* first major loss of the Battle of Britain. The two Hurricanes had been downed (by Horst Tietzen and Josef Fözö) over the north Kent coast while II./JG 51 was covering a late afternoon raid by Dornier bombers heading for Hornchurch airfield, in Essex.

Shortly afterwards, however, while the German formation was still over the Thames Estuary, another Hurricane squadron waded into the fray, quickly sending both Hauptmann Horst Tietzen and one of his 5. *Staffel* pilots down into the sea. Tietzen's recent victim had been his 20th kill of the war.

. . . before taxiing out from his sandbagged revetment at Marquise-West for another cross-Channel mission

Despite the 18 victory bars decorating the tailfin of his *Emil,* Hauptmann Tietzen is caught in unguardedly pensive mood during the afternoon of 16 August. Two days later he would be reported missing over the Thames Estuary

Also aloft over Kent on 18 August, III./JG 51 had been credited with nine victories. The last of them – a Hurricane caught over mid-Channel – had likewise taken Hauptmann Walter Oesau's total to 20. This number of kills was still the yardstick that had won Werner Mölders the *Jagdwaffe's* first Knight's Cross back in May. And on 20 August Oesau and Tietzen (the latter posthumously) duly became the first members of JG 51 to be awarded the coveted decoration.

It is also worth mentioning here that 48 hours later, although no longer *Kommodore* of JG 51, the recently promoted Generalmajor Theo Osterkamp was similarly honoured with the Knight's Cross.

The newly awarded Knight's Cross all but obscures the *Pour le Mérite* worn by the now Generalmajor Theo Osterkamp

Another 'weeping raven' bites the dust. RAF pilots inspect 'Yellow 10' of 6./JG 51, which Oberfeldwebel Fritz Beeck belly-landed alongside the Dover-Deal road on 24 August. The three victory bars on the tailfin refer to Beeck's earlier kills in the Battle of Britain. The fourth, a Hurricane, he had just claimed east of Margate

During the closing days of August, JG 51 was heavily involved in operations over southeast England. But it was also a time of change for the *Geschwader*, for Göring had by now begun his purge of veteran fighter *Kommodores*. And Hauptmann Hannes Trautloft, *Gruppenkommandeur* of III./JG 51, was one of the so-called 'Young Turks' selected to instil some 'much-needed fire' – Göring's phrase – into *Jagdwaffe* operations.

On 24 August Trautloft duly took over from Major Martin Mettig at the head of JG 54, the *Geschwader* with which he will always be associated (see *Osprey Aviation Elite Units 6* for further details). The new *Kommandeur* of III./JG 51 was Hauptmann Walter Oesau, ex-*Kapitän* of 7. *Staffel*.

The following day Major Mölders' *Stab* JG 51 moved from Wissant, the base they had occupied since *'Adler Tag'*, to Pihen, where it would remain alongside I. *Gruppe* for the final stages of the Battle of Britain.

On that same 25 August, the latest in a long line of transient *Jagdgruppen* that had served on a temporary basis under *Stab* JG 51 during the Battles of France and Britain arrived at nearby Marquise-West. But I./JG 77 was to prove different from all the others. Before the year was out it would be incorporated into the *Geschwader* as IV./JG 51. The *Gruppe's* previous history therefore merits brief description.

Its origins can be traced back to that fountainhead of all Luftwaffe fighter units, *Jagdgeschwader* 132 *'Richthofen'* (see *Osprey Aviation Elite Units 1 - Jagdgeschwader 2 'Richthofen'* for further details). The *Gruppe* itself first saw the light of day at Werneuchen on 1 July 1938 as IV./JG 132. It was made up of one *Staffel* detached from I./JG 132 at Döberitz and two *Staffeln* drawn from the ranks of Werneuchen's resident fighter training school, JFS 1.

The school's commander, one Oberleutnant Theo Osterkamp, was initially named as *Kommandeur* of the new *Gruppe*, but his tenure of office lasted only a few days. Deemed to be doing too important a job at the Werneuchen school, Osterkamp was returned to his training duties and Hauptmann Johannes Janke took over IV./JG 132 in his stead. Incidentally, one of Janke's original *Staffelkapitäne* was a certain Oberleutnant Hannes Trautloft. Like the pre-war RAF, the Luftwaffe's fighter arm of the late 1930s was somewhat akin to a private flying club, where almost everyone knew – or knew of – everybody else.

Formed at a time when tension was mounting over the disputed Sudetenland areas of Czechoslovakia, IV./JG 132 was transferred down to Oschatz, in Saxony, on 1 September 1938. And after the signing of the Munich Agreement at the end of that month, which ceded the Sudentenland to Hitler, the *Gruppe* moved into the newly acquired territories, first to Karlsbad and thence to Mährisch-Trübau. It was at the latter field, on 2 November 1938, that the unit underwent redesignation to become I./JG 331.

The *Gruppe's* many moves in its formative weeks were purportedly the reason for the adoption of a worn-out boot as the unit badge. They also gave rise to its unofficial nickname as the *'Wanderzirkus Janke'*, or 'Janke's Travelling Circus'! By early 1939 the *Gruppe* was on the move again, and a further redesignation on 1 May, while based at Breslau-Schöngarten, saw its emergence as I./JG 77.

On 26 August 1939 Hauptmann Janke's *Gruppe* transferred to Juliusburg, in Lower Silesia, in preparation for the invasion of Poland. Its task in the forthcoming campaign would be to fly *freie Jagd* and escort missions ahead of the 8. *Armee* as it advanced out of Silesia northeastwards towards the Polish capital, Warsaw. True to its nickname, I./JG 77 moved base four times in less than three weeks while discharging these duties.

The ground personnel were undoubtedly kept busier than the pilots, for the latter encountered little opposition in the air. The *Gruppe's* three aerial kills of the campaign – all claimed within the first week – included firsts for both Hauptmann Hannes Trautloft and 2. *Staffel* pilot Leutnant Karl-Gottfried Nordmann. The unit's only loss was a Bf 109 written off in a belly landing after being damaged by enemy ground fire.

By 24 September – the day after Hannes Trautloft had been posted away to become *Kommandeur* of I./JG 20 – the *'Wanderzirkus Janke'* was back at Breslau-Schöngarten. Its pilots were not allowed to cool their heels

A shirt-sleeved Hauptmann Hannes Trautloft addresses the assembled groundcrews of his 2./JG 77 prior to the invasion of Poland. In the background, the *Kapitän's* 'Red 1' displays a wealth of interesting markings, including the *Gruppe's* white 'worn-out boot' emblem on the cowling and small circle behind the *Balkenkreuz*. The latter, like the two bands around the aft fuselage (used briefly to denote a formation leader's machine), are also in the *Staffel* colour red

I./JG 77's first victory in Poland – a PZL P-43, downed on 3 September – was claimed by Leutnant Karl-Gottfried Nordmann. It was drinks all round when the future Oak Leaves winner returned to base at Juliusburg and reported his success

for long. On 28 September they were on their travels again, transferring via Oedheim to Frankfurt/Rhein-Main on the western front. The Phoney War, like the campaign in Poland, would see their ground movements outnumber their successes in the air.

During this period the *Gruppe* occupied no fewer than seven bases – coming under the control of JGs 53, 2 and 77 in the process – and was credited with just two kills. The first of these had been a French reconnaissance Mureaux 115 claimed over the Rhine southwest of Karlsruhe on 11 October 1939 by Oberleutnant Ekkehard Priebe, who had taken over 2. *Staffel* from the departed Hannes Trautloft. The second was an RAF Blenheim caught over Aachen by 1./JG 77's Feldwebel Gotthard Goltzsche on 3 January 1940.

By early 1940 I./JG 77's *Emils* had also been transformed by a coat of *hellblau* paint. Here they provide a backdrop as Hauptmann Johannes Janke (left) discusses matters with three of his pilots

With preparations complete for the *Blitzkrieg* in the west, groundcrews of I./JG 77 found different ways to while away the final hours at Odendorf. Some were content simply to sit around and chat . . .

I./JG 77 fought the first fortnight of the *Blitzkrieg* in the west under its parent *Stab* JG 77. And with only one move in that time – the unit transferred forward from its jumping-off point at Odendorf, near Bonn, to Hargimont, in Belgium, on 14 May – the *Gruppe* were able to show what it was really capable of, claiming nearly two dozen victories against a single pilot wounded and two temporarily missing.

Then, on 22 May, well before *'Fall Gelb'* had run its full course, I./JG 77 unexpectedly received orders to return to the Reich to take up defence duties. For the next three months it was back to the old ways for Hauptmann Janke and his pilots as they divided their time and their strength – without any tangible results whatsoever – firstly between three fields in the Berlin area, and then on another three along the North Sea

. . . while the more energetic preferred to kick a football about

coast. It was from two of the latter (Aalborg, in Denmark, and Wyk, on the island of Föhr) that the *Gruppe* rejoined forces to fly to Marquise-West, in the Pas de Calais, on 25 August and finally come under the control of *Stab* JG 51.

There had been no let up in the cross-Channel offensive. On 24 August all three of Werner Mölders' *Gruppen* had again been in action, claiming 16 RAF fighters destroyed. But these successes were beginning to come at a higher cost, for although II./JG 51's eight victories over Kent more than outweighed its own losses of one pilot wounded and one in British captivity, III. *Gruppe* did not escape so lightly. The latter unit's rather dubious claims for a 'P-36' (possibly a Spitfire) and a brace of Defiants were matched by one pilot killed and two missing – the latter pair as a result of a mid-air collision during a dogfight off Ramsgate.

Two days later II./JG 51 was credited with another six victories over the Dover-Canterbury areas of Kent, plus a seventh off the French coast. But these were to be the *Gruppe's* last successes for some weeks, as it was pulled out of the Battle of Britain at the end of the month. Returning to Germany, it was assigned to North Sea coastal defence duties under the control of *Stab* JG 1.

26 August had also seen the first victory for Werner Mölders since his decidedly shaky start off Dover nearly a month earlier. But from this point onwards the *Kommodore's* score would begin to climb steadily – sometimes two or three in a single day – as he maintained his position as the Luftwaffe's most successful fighter pilot, keeping just ahead of his great friend, and rival, Major (later Oberstleutnant) Adolf Galland of neighbouring JG 26.

I. *Gruppe's* 11 victories on 31 August were achieved without casualties. The attached I./JG 77, flying its first operations of the Battle of Britain, was not so fortunate. Despatched on a series of *freie Jagd* and bomber escort missions over Kent and Essex, the *'Wanderzirkus'* claimed four RAF fighters, including a pair of Hurricanes for Oberleutnant Karl-Gottfried Nordmann, recently appointed *Kapitän* of 3. *Staffel.* But it cost the *Gruppe* one pilot killed and five more shot down and captured. Among the latter were Johannes Janke's two other *Staffelkapitäne*, Jürgen Ehrig and Ekkehard Priebe of 1. and 2./JG 77 respectively.

A sixth pilot, future Knight's Cross winner Feldwebel Adolf Borchers, was lucky to escape the same fate. Although his *Emil* was also badly damaged in the sprawling dogfight above the Thames Estuary, he managed to nurse the fighter back to the French coast before ditching and being rescued.

The Battle of Britain continued unabated throughout the first week of September, with Mölders and his pilots claiming some two dozen victories at minimal loss to themselves. It was at this juncture, however, that the Luftwaffe leadership – unaware of just how close they were to attaining their objective of overwhelming the RAF's defences – suddenly switched tactics to an all-out attack on London.

This provided the respite that Fighter Command's airfields in southern England so desperately needed, and was a turning point in the Battle. The German change of policy was partially political. Hitherto Hitler had expressly forbidden any attacks on London. But an RAF bombing raid on his own capital, Berlin, on the night of 25/26 August (itself carried out in response to bombs dropped 'inadvertently' on London 24 hours earlier) helped change the *Führer's* mind. On 2 September he personally gave orders for 'the start of the reprisal raids against London'.

Major Mölders and his three *Gruppen* formed part of the huge fighter umbrella that escorted a solid phalanx of Luftwaffe bombers to London in the first of these raids five days later. They expected to meet fierce opposition, but a number of RAF ground controllers, presuming this to be yet another strike against Fighter Command's airfields, were caught off guard. Many bombers attacked their targets unopposed, and in the fierce dogfights that erupted as the bombers wheeled away from London towards the safety of the coast, JG 51's fortunes again varied considerably.

The *Kommodore* claimed a Spitfire over the capital. And a single Spitfire was all that I. *Gruppe* was able to bring down, for which they paid with one pilot missing and two forced to parachute into captivity. By contrast, III./JG 51 and I./JG 77 were credited with eight and seven victories respectively. It cost each of them one pilot shot down and captured.

I./JG 51 fared better over the Channel and southeast coast of England during the next two days. Its total of eight kills included two that took

'Vati' Mölders always had time for his men. Here he chats to 2. *Staffel's* Oberfeldwebel Fritz Ströhlein, who would disappear during the first major raid on London on 7 September 1940 . . .

both Oberleutnant Richard Leppla and Leutnant Heinz Bär into double figures. But on 11 September the *Gruppe* lost 13-victory Hauptmann Ernst Wiggers, *Kapitän* of 2. *Staffel*, shot down in flames over Lewes (the same Hurricane squadron claimed a pilot of II. *Gruppe* near Wadhurst 30 minutes later). Wiggers' place at the head of 2./JG 51 was taken by Oberleutnant Viktor Mölders, who had flown as a Bf 110 *Zerstörer* pilot in the Polish, Scandinavian and French campaigns, before joining JG 51 to serve under his elder brother.

Four days later the Luftwaffe returned *en masse* to London. 15 September 1940 – now celebrated annually by the British as 'Battle of Britain Day' – witnessed *Reichsmarschall* Göring's last major throw of the dice in his daylight campaign against the RAF. JG 51 claimed 15 kills (including three by I./JG 77) in clashes stretching from the Kent coast to the capital. Its own losses were two pilots killed and one captured.

Historic as 15 September may now be in retrospect, of far greater import to members of JG 51 at the time were the events of 20 September,

. . . while the ramrod posture adopted by Hauptmann Ernst Wiggers, *Staffelkapitän* of 2./JG 51, would suggest that this exchange was on an altogether more formal level. Wiggers was killed in action over Lewes on 11 September. His replacement at the head of 2. *Staffel* was the *Kommodore's* younger brother Victor, who would forced-land his damaged *Jabo* near Winchelsea exactly four weeks later

when the second of a brace of Spitfires from No 92 Sqn shot down over Dungeness took their *Kommodore's* total to 40. Werner Mölders was immediately summoned to Berlin, where he was informed that he had been awarded the Oak Leaves to his Knight's Cross. The presentation would be made by Hitler himself the following day.

Mölders was only the second member of the Wehrmacht to receive the Oak Leaves (the first had been the 'Hero of Narvik', General of Mountain Troops Eduard Dietl). The award set a new benchmark for fighter pilots. If 20 victories won them the Knight's Cross – and the *Geschwader's* third such decoration had just gone to Oberleutnant Hermann-Friedrich Joppien, the *Kapitän* of 1. *Staffel*, for his two Spitfires claimed on 'Battle of Britain Day' – then double that number would now assure them of the Oak Leaves. Adolf Galland was to receive his on 25 September.

With his bombers increasingly operating under cover of darkness, Göring sought new ways of taking the fight to the RAF by day. Fighter sweeps on their own would not be sufficient to lure the opposition up into

Formality was also the order of the day when the Supreme Commander of the *Wehrmacht* presented Major Werner Mölders with the Oak Leaves in the new Reich's Chancellery building in Berlin on 23 September. The moment was captured on film and provided the front cover for the 3 October issue of the popular *Berliner Illustrirte Zeitung*

Once the ceremony was over, a smiling Adolf Hitler took the opportunity to quiz his 'favourite fighter pilot' on the progress of the air war on the Channel front

Hauptmann Hermann-Friedrich Joppien is seen here in March 1941 wearing the Knight's Cross awarded on 16 September 1940

battle (as the RAF was to discover over France the following year). Early in October he therefore ordered that a third of his Channel-based fighter strength be converted to the *Jabo*, or fighter-bomber, role.

In line with most of the *Jagdgeschwader* in the area, each of Mölders' three *Gruppen* offered up a *Staffel* for conversion into fighter-bombers. Just how the selection was made is unclear, but the three involved were 2. and 9./JG 51 and 1./JG 77. The pilots of the latter pair spent a few days at the beginning of October with the *Jabo* experts of *Erprobungsgruppe* 210 at Denain, where their *Emils* were fitted with ventral racks and they received some basic instruction in the techniques of fighter-bombing.

One source suggests that Oberleutnant Viktor Mölders' 2. *Staffel* enjoyed no such luxury. Its machines were converted *in situ* at Pihen, and the pilots had to learn their new art 'on the job', their first sorties being flown over Kent and Greater London on 2 October. Nor can it have been of much comfort to the bomb carriers of 2./JG 51 when others of I. *Gruppe* began to receive the first of the new Bf 109F-1s later in the month.

The first week of October saw some organisational changes within Mölders' command. On the 2nd Hauptmann Johannes Janke's I./JG 77 was detached and placed under the control of JG 54, headquartered at nearby Campagne-lès-Guines. But then, three days later, II./JG 51 – relieved of its fruitless North Sea defence duties under *Stab* JG 1 – returned to the fold, taking up residence at Mardyck, close to Dunkirk. It had hardly touched down before the *Emils* of 5./JG 51 were each being fitted with a rack to carry a 250-kg bomb and Oberleutnant Hans Kolbow was informed that henceforth his *Staffel* was to fly *Jabo* missions.

Although usually operating at high altitudes, the *Jabostaffeln* were far from immune from losses. And, ironically, their first casualty was 2./JG 51's *Staffelkapitän*, Oberleutnant Viktor Mölders, who, together

'Black men' prepare to bomb-up a Bf 109E-4/B *Jabo* of 2./JG 51 at Pihen

One of a series of pictures purportedly taken on the occasion of Werner Mölders' half-century. If this is indeed the case, everybody appears to be rather glum - particularly visiting *Jafü* 'Onkel Theo' Osterkamp, to whom Mölders is reporting. Between the two is JG 51's first Knight's Cross winner, Hauptmann Walter Oesau, now *Kommandeur* of III. *Gruppe*

with one of his pilots, was brought down in a dogfight with Hurricanes over the south coast on 7 October.

By contrast, Werner Mölders was going from strength to strength. He was responsible for all but one of the *Stab's* 13 victories in October. The second of three Hurricanes claimed in as many minutes northwest of Maidstone on the afternoon of 22 October gave the *Kommodore* his half-century. This milestone – Mölders was the first pilot to reach 50 – not only resulted in another mention by name in the *Wehrmacht's* daily news bulletin (and some memorable celebrations at Pihen!), but also no doubt contributed towards his promotion to oberstleutnant three days later.

But for the bulk of the *Geschwader* October proved very much an anti-climax after the great set-piece battles of August and September. I. and III./JG 51 were able to achieve just eight victories each during the course of the month (exactly half of the latter's kills going to *Kommandeur* Hauptmann Walter Oesau, thereby taking his score to 38). Their casualties, however, were disproportionate. Oesau's III. *Gruppe* lost two pilots to British captivity, while I./JG 51 suffered five captured and one – *Gruppenadjutant* Oberleutnant Ernst Terry – killed.

Perhaps refreshed from their enforced North Sea sojourn, II./JG 51 was by far the most successful of the three *Gruppen* during October. Hauptmann Matthes' pilots were credited with a total of 26 enemy aircraft destroyed. The single Hurricane downed over Tunbridge Wells on 17 October provided victory 20 for the *Kapitän* of 6. *Staffel*, Oberleutnant Josef Priller. He received the Knight's Cross 48 hours later.

The *Geschwader's* sole loss on 15 October was Unteroffizier Erich Höhn of 4./JG 51, who baled out of his 'White 2' (a Bf 109E-1, shown here on routine patrol earlier in the year) over Lamberhurst, in Kent

But the *Gruppe's* losses were also the highest of the month – six pilots killed and one captured.

November's worsening weather resulted in a further marked reduction in aerial activity. The 8th was to prove the *Geschwader's* most successful day of the entire month, with the pilots of I./JG 51 claiming three Hurricanes without loss on each of two separate sweeps over the south coast. One of the RAF fighters had fallen to *Kommandeur* Oberleutnant

Ten days later four more pilots joined Erich Höhn in British captivity. Hauptmann Hans Asmus of the *Geschwaderstab* was flying the *Kommodore's* reserve machine when he was shot down by Hurricanes over Marden. The aircraft in question, seen here with Werner Mölders preparing for another mission, was a Bf 109E-4/N which still displayed traces of its original factory-applied code – CI+EC – beneath the *Kommodore's* chevron and bars insignia

One of III. *Gruppe's* two losses on 25 October was Feldwebel Wilhelm Koslowski (centre) of 7./JG 51, who was forced to bale out of his burning *Emil* near Hastings while on a *freie Jagd* sweep. Typical of the many now forgotten names who made up the bulk of the *Geschwader's* Battle of Britain casualties, Koslowski's single success had been a No 107 Sqn Blenheim downed near St Omer on 30 June

Hermann-Friedrich Joppien, who had taken over the *Gruppe* after Hauptmann Hans-Heinrich Brustellin's transfer to the command of I./JG 53 three weeks earlier. Three more of the day's Hurricanes had been credited to Oberleutnant Georg Claus – a great personal friend of Mölders, and hitherto his *Geschwader-Adjutant* – who had now replaced Joppien at the head of 1. *Staffel*.

Further leadership changes took place on 10 November when 3. *Staffel's* Richard Leppla was promoted to hauptmann and given command of III./JG 51 in place of Hauptmann Walter Oesau, who left the *Geschwader* to head III./JG 3. Leppla's position as *Staffelkapitän* of 3./JG 51 was in turn taken by Oberleutnant Heinrich Krafft.

I./JG 51 were credited with another four victories during a major anti-convoy operation over the Thames Estuary on 11 November, but this time

Unlike Asmus and Koslowski, both of whom took to their parachutes, 3./JG 77's Gefreiter Karl Raisinger belly-landed his *Emil* near Brighton after it had suffered engine and radiator damage during a *Jabo* escort mission to London on 25 October. 'Brown 13' was later put on display, its one bent propeller bearing witness to its enforced dead-stick arrival

Another visitor unbidden to these shores was Leutnant Wolfgang Teumer of 2./JG 51, who force-landed his damaged *Jabo* on Manston airfield on 27 November. Rather than being put on display, Teumer's 'Black 12' was restored to flying condition for evaluation purposes. As DG200, it was first flown by the RAF's Enemy Aircraft Flight on 25 February 1941. Today returned to Luftwaffe livery (and with a replacement tail unit), this machine *is* on display – as part of the Battle of Britain collection at the RAF Museum, Hendon

it cost them two 1. *Staffel* pilots, including recently appointed *Kapitän*, Oberleutnant Georg Claus. Also involved in the dogfighting off the north Kent coast, III./JG 51 claimed a solitary Spitfire, but lost one of its own number. Worse was to follow.

The *Gruppe's* air-sea rescue aircraft, an Fw 58 'Weihe', was despatched to the estuary to search for the missing pilots. It was pounced upon by a section of Hurricanes and shot down with the loss of all three crew members. Some sources have suggested that Oberleutnant Claus was leading JG 51 in the *Kommodore's* stead on this date, and that it was Mölders – forbidden to fly by the Medical Officer, but blaming himself for his friend's failure to return – who had personally ordered the rescue attempts.

On 19 November the *Geschwader* bade farewell to another of its early stalwarts when 6. *Staffel's* Oberleutnant Josef Priller departed to take command of 1./JG 26.

Forty-eight hours later Hauptmann Janke's I./JG 77 returned to Guise after its seven-week stint under *Stab* JG 54. Upon arrival, the *Wanderzirkus'* was immediately redesignated as IV./JG 51, thus making Major Werner Mölders' command unique among the frontline *Jagdgeschwader* of this period by being the only one to consist of four component *Gruppen*. During its time with JG 54, the *Gruppe* had been able to claim 26 victories against one pilot killed and two taken into captivity. It was far less successful in its first weeks as IV./JG 51, however. By the end of November it had already lost one pilot killed and another captured, with nothing to show in return.

I./JG 51, which had started the month so well, ended it on an even worse note. Setting out on a raid across the Straits of Dover on 27 November, the *Jabos* of 2. *Staffel* were intercepted by three squadrons of Spitfires. Two of the bomb-carrying *Emils* were shot into the sea, taking their pilots with them. A third made a forced landing on Manston airfield. Part of the fighter-bombers' escort, 3./JG 51 suffered exactly the same number of casualties – two pilots killed and one captured.

November had been an entirely barren month for Werner Mölders, a bad dose of influenza having kept him off operations for much of the time. But on 1 December he claimed one of a pair of Hurricanes encountered over Ashford – the second was credited to his wingman, Oberleutnant Hartmann Grasser. In fact, of the two No 253 Sqn

Major Werner Mölders and wingman Oberleutnant Hartmann Grasser ready for another cross-Channel foray

A Bf 109F of I./JG 51 in its camouflaged hangar at Abbeville in March 1941. Note the replacement DB 601N engine standing on wooden blocks to the left

machines attacked, Mölders' victim crash-landed but was repairable, while the other returned to base damaged.

On the same date, but in separate incidents, II. and III. *Gruppen* also managed to bring down a single Hurricane apiece. Both went to future Knight's Cross winners, the former taking 4. *Staffel's* Leutnant Erich Hohagen into double figures, and the latter providing victory 13 for *Gruppenkommandeur* Hauptmann Richard Leppla. But on this 1 December, III./JG 51 also suffered the *Geschwader's* last combat fatality of the year when Unteroffizier Walter Miesala of 9. *Staffel* went into the Channel off Dover.

Six days later the entire *Geschwader* was withdrawn from the Pas de Calais and sent back to the homeland for rest and refit. *Stab*, I., II. and IV. *Gruppen* all spent the next two months together at Mannheim-Sandhofen, with III./JG 51 in splendid isolation some 270 km to the north of them at Gütersloh.

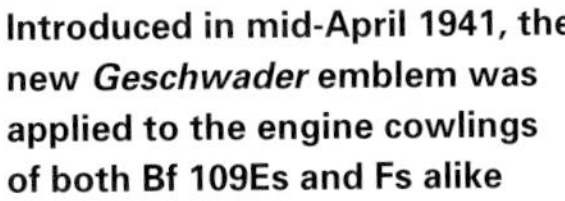

Introduced in mid-April 1941, the new *Geschwader* emblem was applied to the engine cowlings of both Bf 109Es and Fs alike

Oberstleutnant Mölders and his *Geschwaderstab* were the first to return to the Channel front, flying in to Mardyck on 5 February 1941. Four days later I. and IV./JG 51 touched down at Abbeville and Le Touquet, respectively. Like the *Stab*, I. *Gruppe* was now flying Bf 109Fs, but IV./JG 51 was still operating E-models, and would not receive its first *Friedrichs* until the following month. The last to arrive, on 14 February, was II./JG 51 – still equipped with *Emils* – which joined the *Stab* at Mardyck, and III./JG 51, whose mix of Bf 109Es and Fs took up residence at nearby St Omer-Wizernes.

But the war they came back to was very different from the one they had been waging the previous autumn. The RAF had strengthened its defences (in fact, its stance could now be more accurately described as *offensive*), and for the next three months Mölders and his pilots would find themselves operating mainly over the open waters of the Channel – and more often than not closer to the French coast than the English. Incursions into enemy territory were few and far between.

Werner Mölders' first kill since his return to the Pas de Calais (victory 56, claimed on 10 February 1941) was typical of what lay ahead for the *Geschwader* – a Hurricane downed five kilometres to the northeast of Calais. During its remaining time at Mardyck, *Stab* JG 51 would be credited with another two dozen fighters. Exactly half of that number fell to the *Kommodore*, taking Oberstleutnant Mölders' total to 68.

And it was *Kommandeur* Joppien who gained the lion's share of *his* unit's kills, claiming 12 of the 20 victories that would be credited to I./JG 51 in the coming weeks. Among the 12 was Joppien's 40th. Identified as a Hurricane (but possibly a Spitfire) downed northwest of Ashford on 21 April, it resulted in the award of the Oak Leaves 48 hours later.

On the occasion of his 49th birthday on 15 April 1941, 'Onkel Theo' Osterkamp entertained his Channel front *Kommodores* at *Jafü* HQ. They are, from left to right, Günther Lützow (JG 3), Adolf Galland (JG 26), Generalleutnant Osterkamp, Günther *Freiherr* von Maltzahn (JG 53) and Werner Mölders (JG 51)

Photographed at a misty Mardyck on 12 March 1941 (hence no *Geschwader* badge on that yellow cowling yet), Werner Mölders' *Friedrich* displays 61 victory bars on its rudder . . .

Still equipped with *Emils*, II./JG 51 were not far behind I. *Gruppe* with 14 claims over the same period. These were more evenly distributed among 13 of the pilots. The only one to be credited with two victories was future Knight's Cross recipient Unteroffizier Wilhelm Mink, whose first was a Blenheim sent down into the Channel on 29 April.

Exactly one month earlier, on 29 March, another as yet unknown NCO had been severely injured in a crash-landing at Mardyck. Fortunately, Gefreiter Anton Hafner made a full recovery. Before his death in action in June 1944 Oberleutnant 'Toni' Hafner would have risen to become the *Geschwader's* most successful pilot, and the only one to top the double century.

But perhaps the most significant event for II./JG 51 at this time was the posting of *Kommandeur* Hauptmann Günther Matthes to the Air Warfare Academy at Berlin-Gatow, and his replacement at the head of the *Gruppe* by Oberleutnant Josef Fözö.

Of Mölders' two remaining *Gruppen*, III./JG 51 claimed just six kills during its three months at St Omer-Wizernes (by the end of which time it had converted fully to Bf 109Fs). IV./JG 51 achieved more than three times that figure with 19 victories, and it also underwent two changes of command.

On 18 February the long-serving Hauptmann Johannes Janke, who had led the *Gruppe* almost since the day it was activated back in July 1938, finally had to take leave of the pilots of his *'Wanderzirkus'* when he was appointed to a staff position. His replacement was to be Oberleutnant Hans-Karl Keitel, formerly the *Kapitän* of 10. *Staffel*. But the luckless Keitel lasted little more than a week. Moments after claiming his eighth victory (a Hurricane over the Straits of Dover on 16 February), he was himself shot down into the Channel by a Spitfire.

. . . just over a month later, on 16 April, and that total has risen to 65, as is more clearly visible in this close-up shot. Just three more victories would be added – one each on 4, 6 and 8 May – before JG 51 turned its back on the English Channel for good

Keitel was in turn replaced by Major Friedrich Beckh, hitherto a member of Mölders' *Stab*, on March 1. The new *Kommandeur* of IV./JG 51 opened his scoring four days later with his first kill – one of a quartet of No 610 Sqn Spitfires downed by the *Gruppe* off Boulogne.

During its second period of deployment in the Pas de Calais area, JG 51 had been credited with a total of 85 enemy aircraft destroyed. It had cost the *Geschwader* six pilots killed in action, one missing and one wounded. But its days of counting successes in tens, and losses individually, were rapidly drawing to a close. During the last week of May and the first week of June 1941, Mölders and his four *Gruppen*, one after the other, turned their backs on the English Channel for the second, and last, time.

They had been recalled once more to Germany. And when they lifted off again only a matter of days later, their course took them eastwards – towards that part of the *Generalgouvernement* (German-occupied Poland) close to the Soviet border due east of Warsaw.

The first half of the *Geschwader's* eight-year history was over. The second half was just about to begin. It would bear no relationship whatsoever to what had gone before.

1

He 51B 'White 1' of Hauptmann Georg Meyer, *Staffelkapitän* 2./JG 135, Bad Aibling, February 1938

2

Bf 109B 'Yellow 7' of 3./JG 135, Wien (Vienna)-Aspern, March 1938

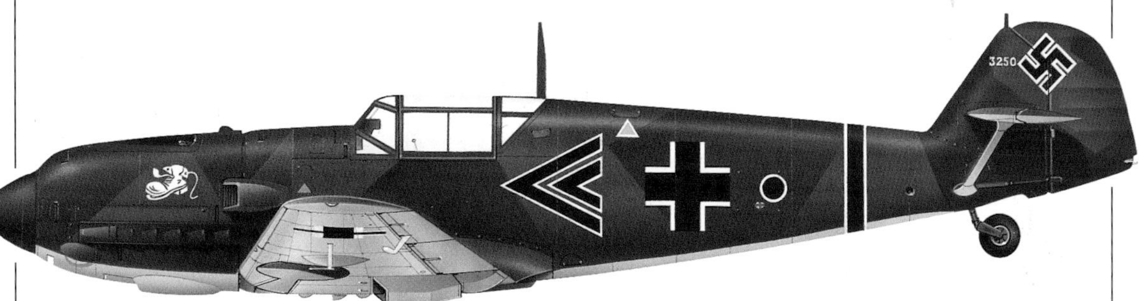

3

Bf 109E-1 'Black Double Chevron' of Hauptmann Johannes Janke, *Gruppenkommandeur* I./JG 77, Kracow/Poland, September 1939

4

Bf 109E-3 'White 1' of Oberleutnant Walter Oesau, *Staffelkapitän* 1./JG 20, Brandenburg-Briest, October 1939

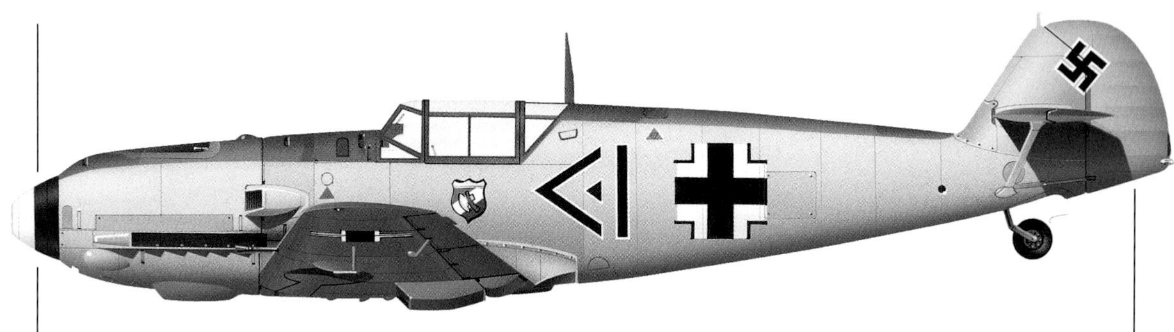

5
Bf 109E 'Black Chevron,Triangle and Bar' I./JG 20, Bönninghardt, March 1940

6
Bf 109E 'White 13' of Feldwebel Heinz Bär, 1./JG 51, Pihen, September 1940

7
Bf 109E 'Black 4' of 5./JG 51, Mardyck, Autumn 1940

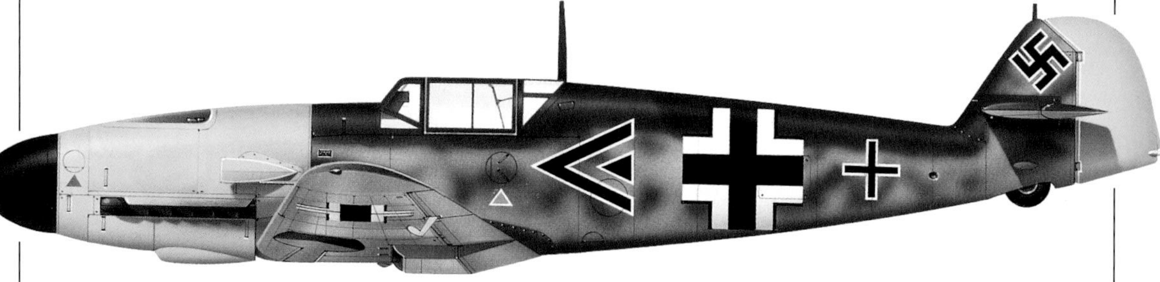

8
Bf 109F 'Black Chevron Triangle' of Major Friedrich Beckh, *Gruppenkommandeur* IV./JG 51, Le Touquet, March 1941

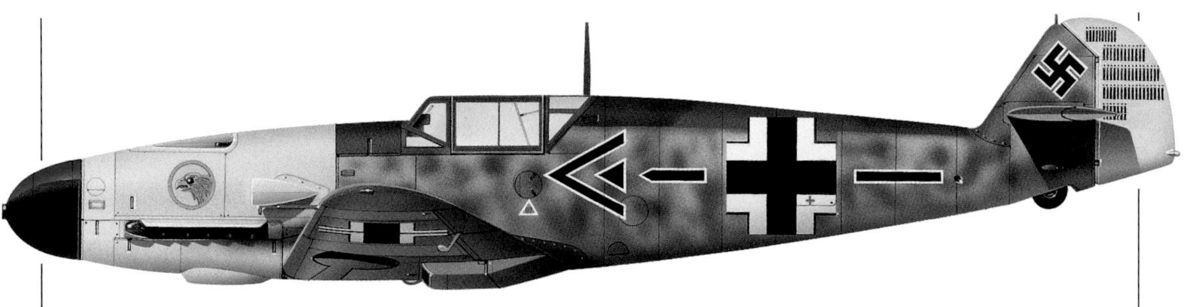

9
Bf 109F 'Black Chevron, Triangle and Bars' of Major Werner Mölders, *Geschwaderkommodore* JG 51, Mardyck 1941

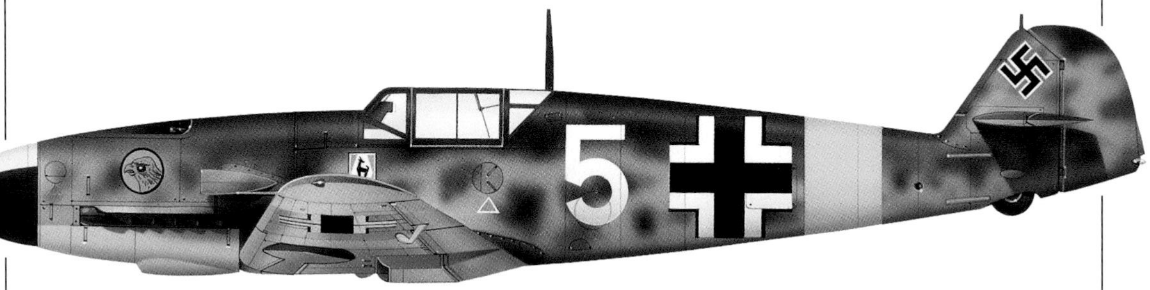

10
Bf 109F-2 'White 5' of Oberfeldwebel Heinrich Höfemeier, 1./JG 51, Starawies/Poland, June 1941

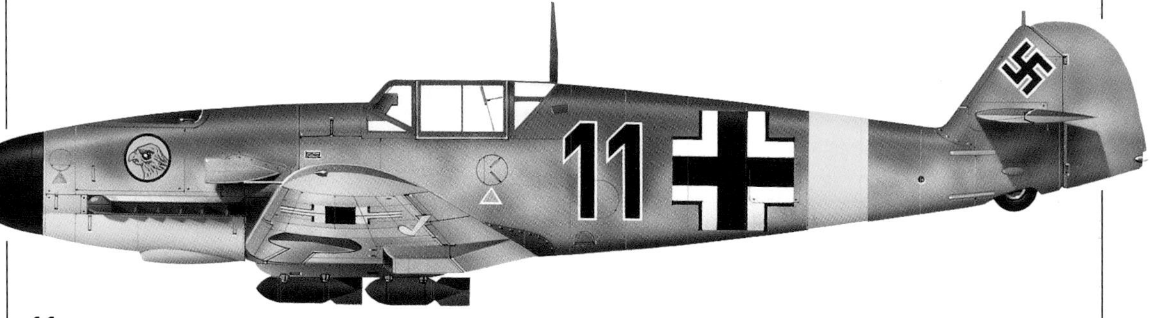

11
Bf 109F-2 'Black 11' of Feldwebel Anton Lindner, 2./JG 51, Stara Bychov, July 1941

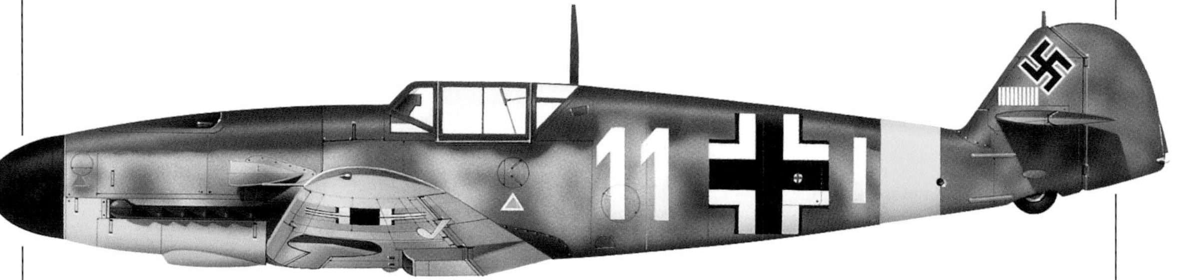

12
Bf 109F-2 'White 11' of Feldwebel Werner Bielefeldt, 7./JG 51, Bobruisk-South, July 1941

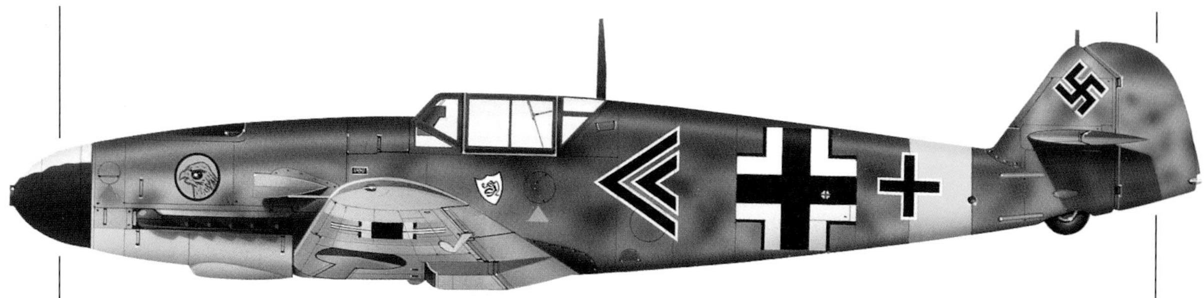

13
Bf 109F-2 'Black Double Chevron' of Oberleutnant Karl-Gottfried Nordmann, *Gruppenkommandeur* IV./JG 51, Shatalovka, August 1941

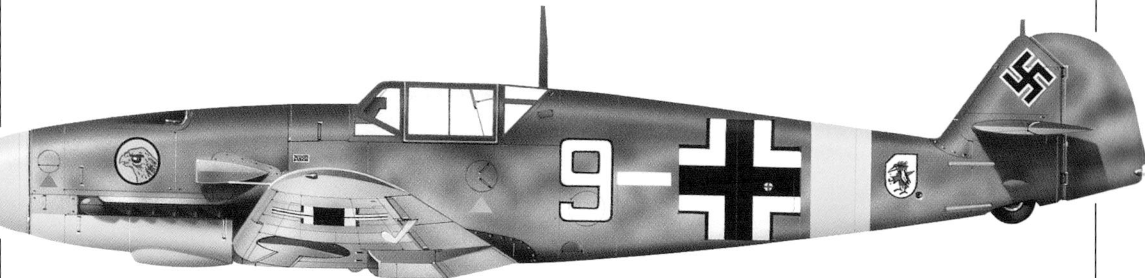

14
Bf 109F 'White 9' of 4./JG 51, Sezhinskaya, September 1941

15
Bf 109F 'Black 10' of Leutnant Hans Strelow, *Staffelkapitän* 5./JG 51, Szolzy, c. February 1942

16
Fw 190A-3 'Black Double Chevron' of Hauptmann Heinrich Krafft, *Gruppenkommandeur* I./JG 51, Jesau/East Prussia, September 1942

17
Fw 190A 'White 9' of Leutnant Oskar Romm, 1./JG 51, Vyazma, October 1942

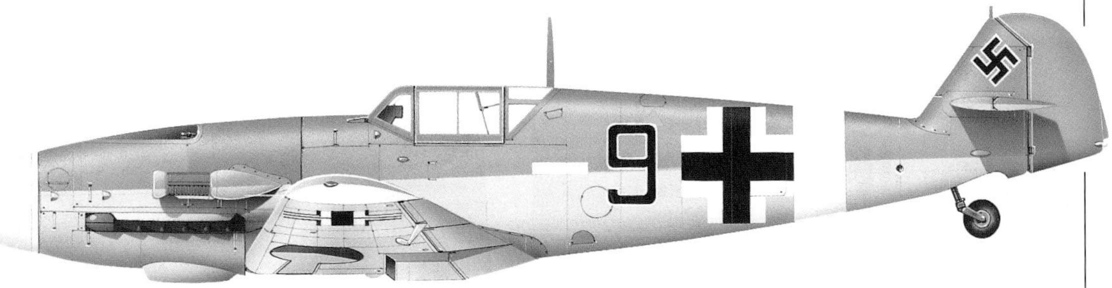

18
Bf 109G-2/trop 'Black 9' of 5./JG 51, Bizerta/Tunisia, November 1942

19
Bf 109G-2/trop 'White 4' of Leutnant Günther Eggebrecht, 6./JG 51, Tunis/El-Aouina, December 1942

20
Fw 190A-3 'Brown 9' of Oberleutnant Heinz Lange, *Staffelkapitän* 3./JG 51, Vyazma, December 1942

21
Fw 190A-4 'White 10' of Unteroffizier Otto Gaiser, 10./JG 51, Bryansk, March 1943

22
Fw 190A-5 'Black Chevron and Triangle' of Major Erich Leie, *Gruppenkommandeur* I./JG 51, Orel, May 1943

23
Fw 190A-4 'Black 4' of 8./JG 51, Orel, July 1943

24
Hs 129B 'White 5' of Pz.J.St/JG 51, Southern Sector, August 1943

25

Fw 190A-6 'Black 8 and Bars' of Stabsstaffel JG 51, Bobruisk, Winter 1943-44

26

Fw 190A-6 'White 14' of Oberfeldwebel Günther Josten, 1./JG 51, Orsha, March 1944

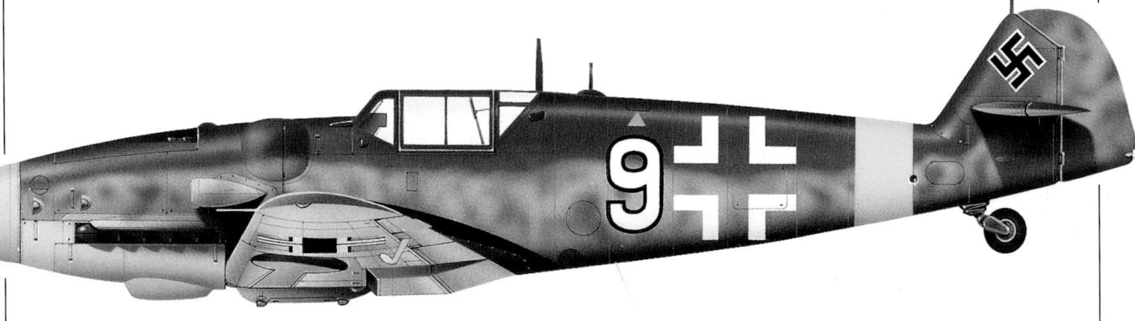

27

Bf 109G-6 'White 9' of Oberfeldwebel Günther Josten, 1./JG 51, Bobruisk, April 1944

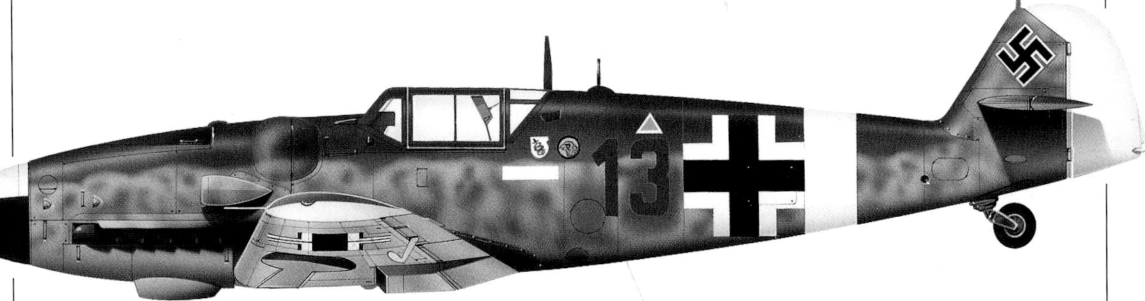

28

Bf 109G-6 'Red 13' of Leutnant Götz Bergmann, 5./JG 51, Gadurra/Rhodes, July 1944

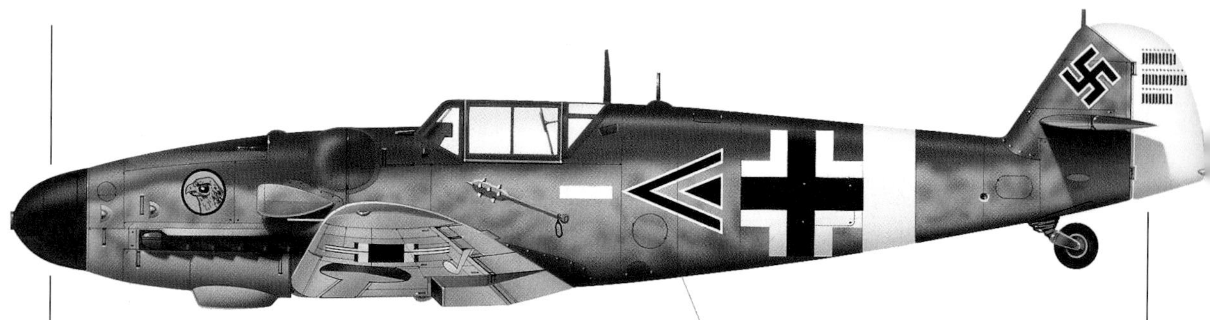

29
Bf 109G-6 'Black Chevron Triangle' of Major Karl Rammelt, *Gruppenkommandeur* II./JG 51, Nis/Yugoslavia, c. August 1944

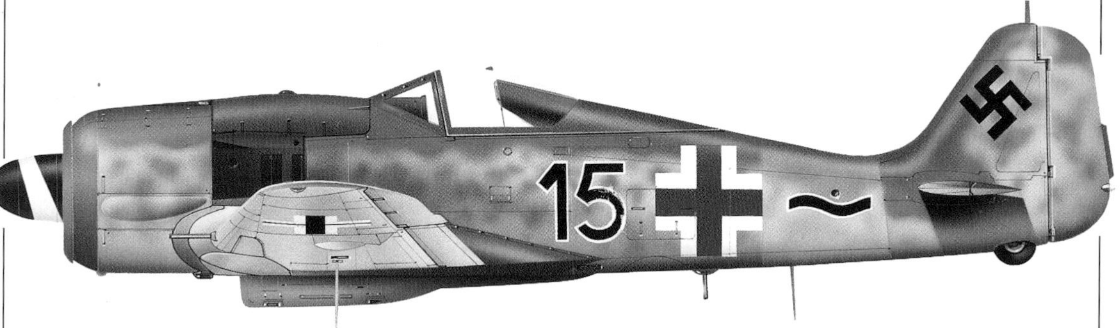

30
Fw 190A-9 'Black 15' of 14./JG 51, Garz/Usedom, April 1945

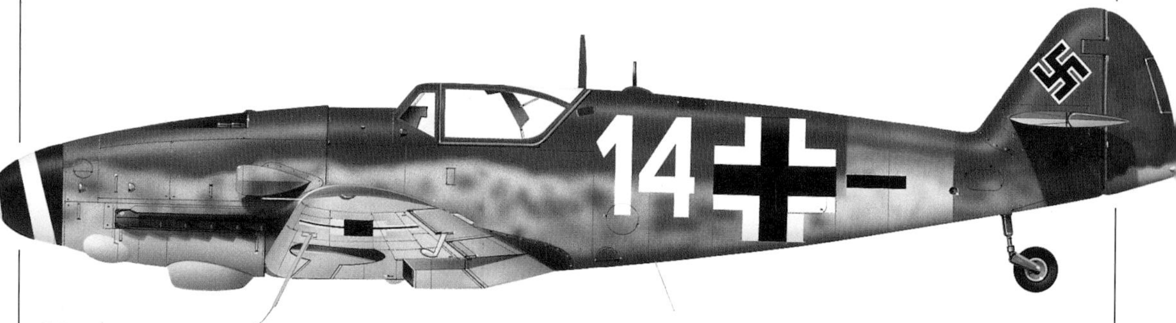

31
Bf 109G-10 'White 14' of Hauptmann Waldemar Wagler, 15./JG 51, Garz/Usedom, April 1941

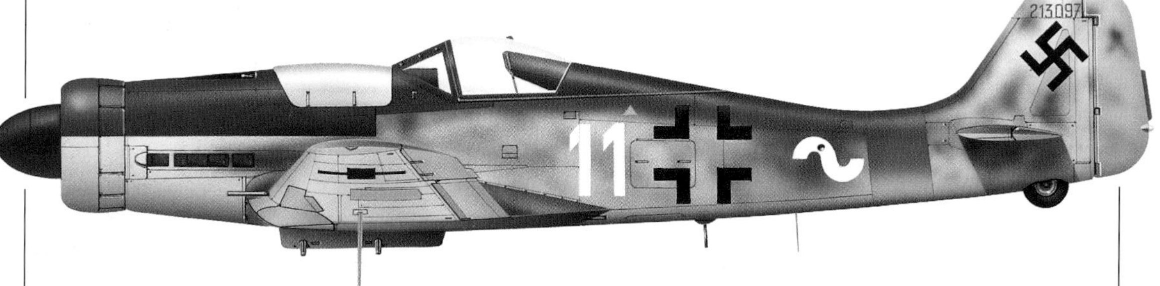

32
Fw 190D-9 'White 11' of 13./JG 51, Flensburg, May 1945

1
JG 51
worn on cowling of Bf 109F/G and Fw 190A

2
I./JG 51 (early)
worn below windscreen of He 51 and Bf 109B/D

3
I./JG 51 (late)
worn below windscreen of Bf 109E/F and Fw 190A

4
II./JG 51 (early)
worn below cockpit of Bf 109D and on aft fuselage of Bf 109D/E

5
II./JG 51 (late)
worn on (right) cowling of Bf 109G

6
III./JG 51 (I./JG20)
worn below cockpit of Bf 109E

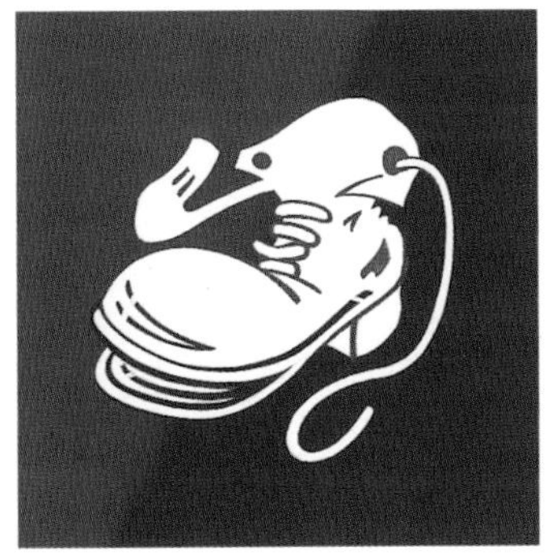

7
7./JG 51 (1./JG 20)
worn on cowling of Bf 109E

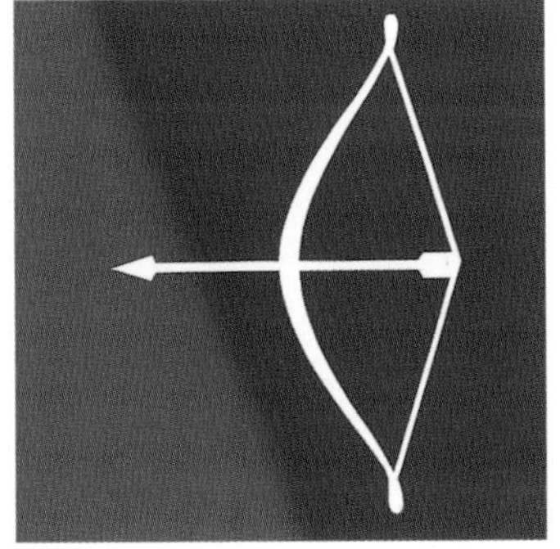

8
8./JG 51 (2./JG 20)
worn on cowling of Bf 109E

9
IV./JG 51 (I./JG 77)
worn on cowling of Bf 109E and (reduced) below cockpit of Bf 109F

EASTERN FRONT 1941-43

Launched in the early hours of 22 June 1941, Operation *Barbarossa* was Hitler's greatest and most ambitious *Blitzkrieg* gamble of all. Its objective was nothing less than the destruction of the Soviet Union, and the timetable was perilously tight, with but five months to go before the expected onset of the Russian winter.

On their cluster of four fields to the east of Warsaw (which they shared with elements of JG 53), Oberstleutnant Werner Mölders' *Gruppen* were almost in the centre of the 4480 km-long front that stretched all the way

Above
Waiting for *Barbarossa* to begin, a group of mechanics, their work done, relax in the shade provided by the wing of this I./JG 51 *Friedrich*, while its pilot (left) snoozes in the sun. The location is a forward landing ground 'somewhere in Poland' – probably Starawies, northeast of Warsaw – in mid-June 1941

Left
3. *Staffel's* Oberfähnrich Hans-Gottfried Schultz is also well away in the comfort of his deck-chair. Yet to score, his first victory would be an Il-2 *Sturmovik* downed southwest of Moscow on 14 October 1941

During the advance on Moscow, JG 51 co-operated closely with the armoured divisions of *Panzergruppe 2*. Here Mölders confers with Generaloberst Heinz Guderian, GOC *Panzergruppe* 2, at an early stage in the campaign. Behind them, wearing Oak Leaves, is Hermann-Friedrich Joppien, while the bulky figure to the left of Mölders – in summer flight blouse and with a mosquito net over his peaked cap – is Josef Fözö

from the Barents Sea in the north to the Black Sea in the south. Their principal task in this new theatre of operations would be to clear the skies above and ahead of the armoured divisions of *Panzergruppe* 2, which itself formed the right-hand flank of Army Group Centre's twin pincer advance aimed northeastwards towards Moscow (whose fall, it was confidently predicted, would immediately bring about the collapse of the Soviet state).

But first, in true *Blitzkrieg* fashion, *Barbarossa* would begin with a series of pre-emptive air strikes intended to eliminate the enemy's air forces on the ground. The results on the opening day exceeded all expectations. By the time darkness fell on 22 June, it was estimated that although more than 300 Soviet aircraft had been shot down, some 1500(!) had been destroyed on the ground. Even Göring refused at first to believe these staggering claims. But, if anything, they were proved to be conservative after German troops had overrun the enemy's frontline areas – including all 31 of the airfields targeted – and a detailed survey of the damage inflicted could be carried out.

It is not known how many Soviet aircraft the *Geschwader* accounted for on the ground, but 2./JG 51, whose new *Friedrichs* – like their earlier *Emils* – had been fitted with ventral bomb racks, were alone credited with 43 destroyed in four separate *Jabo* sorties during the course of the day.

In the air, Mölders' four *Gruppen* (with IV./JG 51 temporarily attached to *Stab* JG 53) claimed no fewer than 93 enemy machines shot down! The *Kommodore* himself was responsible for four of the *Stabsschwarm's* five victories. These took his total to 72, and won him the immediate Swords. The first award of this newly instituted decoration had gone to Adolf Galland, for 69 kills in the west, just 24 hours earlier.

Many other pilots achieved multiple successes during these early hours of *Barbarossa*. Among them was 1./JG 51's Leutnant Heinz Bär, whose trio of kills before mid-morning raised his score to 20. But Bär would have to wait ten days for his Knight's Cross, by which time he had added a further nine to his tally.

The second day of the campaign in the east saw the *Geschwader* carry out another round of low-level strikes, but in stark contrast to the day

The *Kommodore* describes his first eastern front victory – an I-153, downed at 0500 hrs on the opening morning of *Barbarossa*. This victory took Mölders' tally to 69 overall. He would add a trio of SB-2 bombers to his score later that same day

before, it resulted in only two aerial victories. One of these provided a first for future Knight's Cross recipient Feldwebel Anton 'Toni' Lindner of 2./JG 51.

Another 'Toni' opened his shore-sheet 24 hours later. Fully recovered from the injuries he had sustained in the crash-landing at Mardyck three months earlier, the Soviet SB-2 bomber claimed by 6. *Staffel's* Gefreiter Anton 'Toni' Hafner was the first rung on the ladder to his becoming JG 51's top scorer.

In addition to Hafner's opener, the *Geschwader* had been credited with a further 81 victories on that 24 June, for despite the Luftwaffe's best efforts, the Red Air Force was far from being knocked out. Having recovered from the immediate shock of the first days' savage onslaught, Soviet commanders called up bombers from as-yet untouched rear-area bases and hurled them in waves against the advancing German ground forces. With no frontal fighters to protect them, the Soviet bombers suffered horrendous losses. On 25 June JG 51 alone shot down 83 Tupolev SB-2s. And still the desperate Russians kept up the pressure. It peaked on the last day of the month, when Mölders and his *Gruppen* claimed an unprecedented 137 enemy aircraft destroyed!

This huge total included several personal and unit landmark scores. The third of the five Ilyushin DB-3 bombers downed by the *Kommodore* took Werner Mölders' score to 80 – level with *Rittmeister* Manfred *Freiherr* von Richthofen, the legendary 'Red Baron', and top-scoring German fighter pilot of World War 1. Hauptmann Hermann-Friedrich Joppien was also credited with five victories, the fourth of which gave the *Kommandeur* of I. *Gruppe* his half-century.

22 June's four victories earned Werner Mölders the Swords. Here, he chats to Gefreiter Anton Hafner (right), whose first kill was one of the 11 SB-2s brought down by 6./JG 51 on 24 June. In the centre, minus mosquito netting, is Josef 'Joschko' Fözö, *Kommandeur* of II. *Gruppe*

And 30 June 1941 was the date on which it was announced that JG 51 had become the first *Jagdgeschwader* to reach 1000 victories!

By now German forces had already smashed through Soviet frontier defences along the River Bug and breached the more substantial 'Stalin Line' some 300 km inside Russian territory guarding the approaches to Minsk. The fighting around the capital of White Russia resulted in the first of the great 'cauldron' battles of the eastern front. When it ended on 9 July, nearly a third of a million Russian prisoners had been taken.

Once again, regardless of cost, the Soviets had thrown in their unescorted bombers in a vain attempt to blast open an escape route for the survivors of the four Russian armies trapped inside the 'cauldron'. And once again JG 51's pilots had exacted a heavy toll. On 2 July an SB-2 had provided Hauptmann Josef Fözö with victory 22, and the immediate award of the Knight's Cross.

***Friedrichs* of II./JG 51 in their camouflaged dispersal area at Sluzk, a landing strip to the west of Bobruisk, where they spent the week of 28 June through to 4 July 1941**

With the danger of Soviet bombing raids increasing, camouflage became ever more vital. Tucked well under the trees, these machines would have been all but invisible from the air

Minsk lay at the western end of the major Rollbahn, or supply highway, that linked it directly to Moscow. This formed the obvious axis for Army Group Centre's line of advance. And within 24 hours of the collapse of the Minsk 'cauldron', the Army Group's spearheads had captured the town of Vitebsk, nearly a third of the way along the 880-km highway to the Soviet capital.

JG 51's *Gruppen* had already leapfrogged forward four times since the launch of *Barbarossa* in their efforts to keep abreast of General Guderian's Panzers. By 10 July the bulk of the *Geschwader* was gathered on the complex of ex-Soviet airfields around Bobruisk, some way to the south of the Rollbahn. Only Major Beckh's IV./JG 51, still operating under the control of JG 53, was based at Borissov, close to the highway itself.

For the first six weeks of *Barbarossa*, IV. *Gruppe* operated under the control of JG 53. True to its roots, the one-time *'Wanderzirkus'* changed bases no fewer than nine times during that period as it followed the ground forces advancing eastwards along the Minsk-Moscow highway. The 'worn-out boot' emblem was never more apt, albeit now very much reduced in size and carried below the cockpit, as seen here on Oberfeldwebel Heinrich Hoffmann's 'Yellow 4'

Cameras and applause greet Werner Mölders' return to base on 15 July with victories 100 and 101 under his belt

Thus far, the *Geschwader's* losses had been incredibly light. Only five pilots had been reported killed or missing, including one brought down during a low-level attack on a Soviet armoured train. But the many recent moves, coupled with the multiple missions being flown almost daily, were having a serious effect on JG 51's serviceability figures. Many pilots were also beginning to feel the strain. On 11 July the newly decorated 'Joschko' Föző crashed on take-off. His injuries were so severe that he would be off operations for ten months. In the meantime, II./JG 51 would be led by acting *Kommandeure*.

The following day, one of the three kills credited to Hauptmann Richard Leppla gave the *Geschwader* its 500th eastern front victory (and, at the same time, took its overall wartime total to 1200). And in that summer of 1941, the greatest *Experte* of them all was undoubtedly Werner Mölders. On 14 July a trio of Soviet Pe-2 bombers had taken his total to a tantalising 99. Twenty-four hours later, another pair of Petlyakovs assured him a place in military aviation history as the first fighter pilot ever to reach the century!

Having been second in line for both the Oak Leaves and the Swords, Werner Mölders' premier position was now firmly established by the immediate award of the newest and highest grade of the Knight's Cross – the Diamonds. Or, as the special communiqué of 17 July announced in more formal, if somewhat fulsome terms, 'The *Führer* and Supreme Commander of the *Wehrmacht* has awarded Oberstleutnant Mölders, this shining example of Luftwaffe heroism and the most successful fighter pilot in the world, as the first officer in the *Wehrmacht* with Germany's highest medal for bravery, the Oak Leaves with Swords and Diamonds to the Knight's Cross of the Iron Cross'.

Perhaps a trifle unfairly, the celebrations surrounding the *Kommodore's* achievement rather overshadowed the award of the Knight's Cross to the

The *Kommodore's* final wartime tally on the rudder of his *Friedrich*. The 101 kills represented here – all but the first 25 scored with JG 51 – brought to an end Mölders' operational career

One of Oberstleutnant Mölders last sad duties as *Kommodore* of JG 51 was to take the salute as Oberleutnant Hans Kolbow, *Staffelkapitän* of 5./JG 51, was laid to rest with full military honours at II. *Gruppe's* Stara Bychov base on 16 July 1941

The new *Kommandeur* of IV. *Gruppe*, Hauptmann Karl-Gottfried Nordmann (centre), with four of his unit's leading *Experten* at Shatalovka in late July 1941. They are, from left to right, Unteroffizier Franz-Josef Beerenbrock, Oberfeldwebel Heinrich Hoffmann, Hauptmann Nordmann, Leutnant Heinz Bär and Feldwebel Herbert Friebel. Between them, these five would add an astounding 397 victories to the *Geschwader's* collective scoreboard

wounded Hermann Staiger (for his 25 victories) and the loss of Oberleutnant Hans Kolbow, *Kapitän* of 5. *Staffel* (who was killed when his machine was hit by ground fire during a low-level attack, and he baled out at a height of only 20 metres), both on that same 16 July.

But for Werner Mölders the century carried a sting in its tail. He was immediately banned from further operational flying. Promoted to the rank of Oberst on 20 July, he was appointed the Luftwaffe's first *General der Jagdflieger* on 7 August.

If Theo Osterkamp had proven to be a hard act to follow as *Geschwaderkommodore*, then the void left by Mölders' departure would be even harder to fill. The man selected for the task was Major Friedrich Beckh, *Kommandeur* of IV./JG 51, whom Werner Mölders had personally plucked from the semi-obscurity of the General Staff to join the *Geschwaderstab* of JG 51 back in October 1940.

Beckh's assumption of command of JG 51 on 19 July meant a reshuffle in the ranks of IV. *Gruppe*. Oberleutnant Karl-Gottfried Nordmann became the *Kommandeur*, while Nordmann's place at the head of 12. *Staffel* was taken by the up-and-coming Leutnant Heinz Bär.

While the *Geschwader* continued to enjoy successes in the air (albeit now at mounting cost), the ground troops were pushing ever nearer to Moscow. But reports on 16 July that they had captured the next major key point – the city of Smolensk on the River Dnieper, some 370 km from the Russian capital – proved premature. The Germans were driven back, and another huge 'cauldron' battle developed as elements of three more Soviet armies were gradually encircled.

On 27 July, the last of the month's five Knight's Crosses were awarded. One was presented to Hauptmann Richard Leppla, *Kommandeur* of III. *Gruppe*, for 27 victories. The other was conferred posthumously upon Hans Kolbow, who had exactly the same number at the time of his death. Three days later Kolbow's successor as *Kapitän* of 5./JG 51, Leutnant Hans-Joachim Steffens, was killed in action against Soviet bombers north of Bobruisk.

Although the Red Air Force's frontline fighters had been conspicuous mainly by their absence since the opening air strikes of *Barbarossa*, they were now beginning to re-appear. But these newcomers were mostly

JG 51's area of operations on the eastern front in 1941-43 (*map by John Weal*)

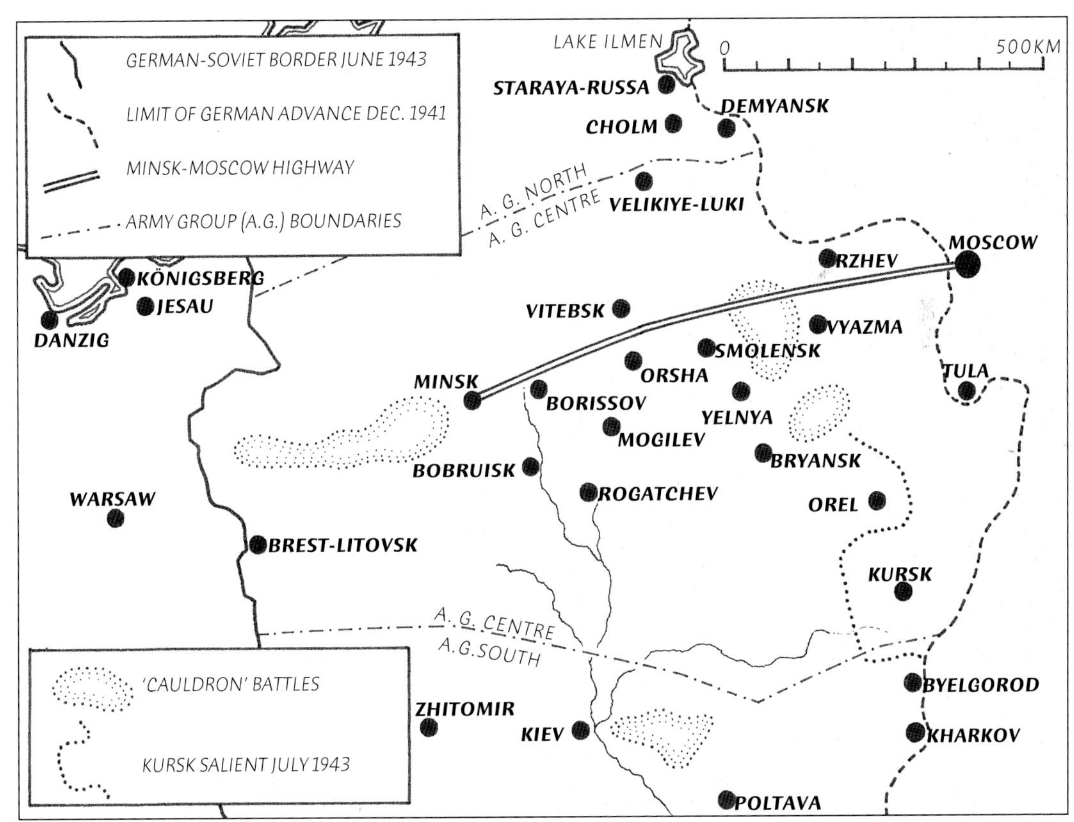

obsolescent Polikarpov types brought up from the rear areas. They were hardly a match for the Luftwaffe's Bf 109s, especially those in the hands of experienced pilots, whose individual scores continued to grow.

In fact, so many fighter pilots were approaching, or passing, the 20-victory benchmark hitherto used in determining the award of the Knight's Cross that there was a very real danger of this prestigious decoration becoming devalued. If many more eastern front pilots reached the previously obligatory 20, it was said, what had once been the Reich's highest medal for valour would soon be little more than a campaign medal! Something had to be done. During the remaining years of the war the total number of kills required to win the Knight's Cross would therefore steadily rise, especially in the east. But the increases were neither strictly incremental, nor did there appear to be any correlation between individual cases.

JG 51's next two Knight's Cross recipients, for example, IV. *Gruppe's* Karl-Gottfried Nordmann and Oberleutnant Karl-Heinz Schnell, *Kapitän* of 9. *Staffel*, were both presented with their awards on 1 August

Oberleutnant Karl-Heinz Schnell, the *Staffelkapitän* of 9./JG 51, wearing the Knight's Cross awarded to him on 1 August 1941

The rudder of Heinz Bär's machine already bears the 60 victory symbols (the last two a pair of Tupolev SB-2 bombers downed on 12 August) that would win him the Oak Leaves two days later. Sharing the joke here is his long-time wingman Heinrich Hoffmann (right), whose 40th on this same 12 August would result in the Knight's Cross. Hoffmann would be honoured with posthumous Oak Leaves after being killed in action against Il-2 *Sturmoviks* south of Yelnya on 3 October

when their scores were standing level at 29 each. Of the following pair, however, decorated 11 days later, 1. *Staffel's* Leutnant Erwin Fleig had 26 kills, whereas Oberfeldwebel Heinrich Hoffmann of 12./JG 51 had just been credited with his 40th.

The criteria for the Oak Leaves were also being upped in similar, seemingly cavalier, fashion. Eleven months earlier, 40 kills had sufficed for the first Oak Leaves to be presented (to Werner Mölders and Adolf Galland). By the time Oberleutnant Heinz Bär's award was announced on 14 August, he had already reached 60. In fact, Bär's 60th had gone down two days before, and the *Kapitän* of 12. *Staffel* had added two more to his total in the interim.

But it was not all successes and celebrations for JG 51 in the summer of 1941. Among August's nine casualties, the most grievous loss was that of Hauptmann Hermann-Friedrich Joppien, *Gruppenkommandeur* of I./JG 51.

On 25 August Joppien and his wingman, Leutnant Erwin Fleig, took off from Miglin, a strip to the northeast of Bobruisk, for a *freie Jagd* sweep ahead of the Panzers advancing on Bryansk. Fleig's combat report describes what happened next;

'About 15 km southwest of Bryansk, Hauptmann Joppien spotted three Pe-2s beneath us to the right, flying in a southwesterly direction. In a wide right-hand curve, we approached the Russian aircraft from below and behind. As we got nearer, we noticed three Russian Type I-16 fighters some 100-200 metres above the bombers to the left. The fighters were at a height of some 500-600 m, and flying 150-200 m apart.

'Hauptmann Joppien gave the order to attack the fighters. He took the right-hand wingman and I took the left-hand one. We attacked from astern and below. Before I had opened fire on the machine flying ahead of me, I saw the fighter attacked by Hauptmann Joppien dive away out of

Friedrichs of the *Gruppenstab* II./JG 51 on a forward landing ground – possibly Shatalovka-West – in the late summer of 1941. The *Gruppe's* white horizontal bar marking is just visible *ahead* of the fuselage cross on the Adjutant's machine in the foreground (see colour profile 14 for a clearer example of this marking)

control to the right, trailing a thick banner of smoke. I did not observe this machine crash, as by now I had opened fire on the fighter in front of me.

'After this had also gone down trailing thick black smoke, I saw Hauptmann Joppien suddenly pull his Bf 109 sharply to the right. I followed his manoeuvre and observed as Hauptmann Joppien, from an altitude of some 600-700 m, went from a steep turn into an uncontrolled dive and, without any attempt at recovery, crashed into the ground. I observed an explosion and fire at the point of impact.

'I was not able to tell whether Hauptmann Joppien had been shot down by the leader of the Russian fighters, or whether he had been hit by fire from one of the bombers flying to the right beneath him.'

The two Polikarpovs had provided victory 28 for Fleig and taken Joppien's tally to 70, making the latter the fourth highest scoring pilot in the Luftwaffe at the time of his death.

Hauptmann Hermann-Friedrich Joppien – who was immediately replaced at the head of I./JG 51 by Hauptmann Wilhelm Hachfeld, formerly *Kapitän* of his 2. *Staffel* – was the first *Gruppenkommandeur* to be killed since Major Burgaller had lost his life in crash on the shores of Lake Constance during the Phoney War. He would not be the last.

The *Kommandeure* of III. and IV. *Gruppen*, Hauptleute Richard Leppla (left) and Karl-Gottfried Nordmann, enjoy a meal together in the *Kasino* (Officers' Mess) of an obviously permanent ex-Red Air Force station – possibly that occupied by *Geschwader* HQ at Kiev in September 1941 – note the unit emblem and portrait of Werner Mölders on the wall

Soviet bombing and strafing attacks were an ever growing threat. 3./JG 51's 'Brown 7' has been riddled by machine gun and cannon fire. This appears to have set the fuel tank on fire, which in turn caused the oxygen cylinders to explode and split the aft fuselage apart

Joppien's loss was almost a portent of things to come. Despite continued individual successes for the *Geschwader*, enemy resistance was stiffening both in the air and on the ground. Smolensk had finally been captured on 14 August, and JG 51's *Gruppen* were now concentrated on fields to the south of the city. But on 30 August (the day 12. *Staffel's* Leutnant Herbert Huppertz was awarded the Knight's Cross) two Soviet armies from the central reserve counter-attacked at Yelnya, less than 60 kilometres ahead of them.

During the first two days of September the *Geschwader's* bases were subjected to a series of heavy bombing raids and strafing attacks. II. *Gruppe* suffered particularly badly. Then, on 7 September, its acting-*Kommandeur*, Oberleutnant Erich Hohagen of 4. *Staffel*, was wounded in a dogfight near Bryansk. He was immediately replaced by another *Staffelkapitän*, 5./JG 51's Oberleutnant Hartmann Grasser, who had received the Knight's Cross just three days earlier.

On 8 September 1941 one of a pair of enemy fighters claimed by the *Kommodore* took the *Geschwader's* collective total to 2000. But on the ground things were not going so well. The drive on Moscow had slowed perceptibly. Instead, attention was now being turned towards the south, where the ill-fated 6. *Armee*, which would be annihilated at Stalingrad, was rapidly approaching Kiev, the capital of the Ukraine.

In mid-September, leaving just I./JG 51 north of the Rollbahn, Major Beckh led the rest of the *Geschwader* (IV. *Gruppe* having been released by JG 53 the previous month) down to two fields northeast of the Ukrainian capital, where another massive 'cauldron' battle was developing. The Bf 109 pilots' primary tasks were to sweep the skies above and around the 'cauldron', and prevent enemy bombers from interfering with the encirclement of almost the entire strength of the Soviet South-Western Front.

The temporary move south was a fateful one for Major Beckh. On 16 September, after accounting for another brace of enemy machines – this time SB-2 bombers – the *Kommodore* was himself hit by ground fire during a low-level attack on Soviet positions. Although severely wounded, he managed to make an emergency landing some 30 kilometres away from base. He was to spend many weeks in hospital, not returning to the *Geschwader* until near the end of December. And even then Beckh was not fit enough to fly operationally. In the meantime, JG 51 would be in the hands of caretaker *Kommodore* Major Günther Lützow, who discharged this additional duty while remaining in command of his own JG 3.

On the day that Beckh was brought down, Oberleutnant Karl-Gottfried Nordmann, the *Kommandeur* of IV. *Gruppe*, received the Oak Leaves for his 59 victories. Forty-eight hours later, on 18 September, the wounded Friedrich Beckh was awarded the Knight's Cross for his 27.

6. *Armee* took Kiev on 19 September, and the great 'cauldron' battle to the east of the city ended a week later with the capture of over two-thirds of a million Soviet troops. By that time, however, JG 51's *Gruppen* had returned to the central sector, where Operation *Taifun* (Typhoon) – the final all-out push for Moscow, involving 14 Panzer, eight mechanised and 56 infantry divisions – was about to begin.

Taifun was launched on 2 October. Weather conditions were perfect – cold but clear. From their bases to the southeast of Smolensk, JG 51 would once again be operating above the armoured divisions of *Panzergruppe* 2 (now renamed 2. *Panzerarmee*). Still forming the outermost right-hand flank of Army Group Centre, the *Panzerarmee's* orders were first to advance on the town of Tula and then wheel due north towards Moscow.

But enemy opposition was immediate and determined. The leading Panzers were subjected to almost continual attack from the air. On only the second day of *Taifun*, Oberfeldwebel Heinrich Hoffmann of 12./JG 51 was reported missing in action against a gaggle of low-flying Il-2 *Sturmovik* assault aircraft. One of the *Geschwader's* highest scorers at the time of his loss (second only to his *Staffelkapitän*, the hospitalised Heinz Bär), Hoffmann would be honoured with posthumous Oak Leaves on 19 October.

The month's three Knight's Crosses were all awarded during the opening stages of *Taifun*. On 5. October Oberleutnant Erich Hohagen, who had been wounded while serving as acting-*Kommandeur* of II. *Gruppe*, received his for 30 victories. Twenty-four hours later, the other two both went to members of IV./JG 51 – 11. *Staffel's* Leutnant Georg Seelmann and Unteroffizier Franz-Josef Beerenbrock of the *Gruppenstab*, for totals of 37 and 42 respectively.

Among 6 October's 18 kills was the *Geschwader's* 1500th Soviet aircraft destroyed. Also on that day, to everyone's astonishment, it began to snow! Fortunately, it did not last long, as a slight rise in the temperature soon turned the snow to rain. But it was, quite literally, a chilling reminder that time was running out.

Nevertheless, sufficient ground was gained during the first week of

While serving as caretaker *Kommodore*, JG 3's Günther Lützow had at his disposal a Bf 109F bearing JG 51's badge and identical command insignia to those of Mölders' earlier *Friedrichs* (see photograph on page 60). The rudder scoreboard, however, was Lützow's own, and included his century victory – an 'I-61' downed on 24 October 1941

Although barely visible here, Franz-Josef Beerenbrock is wearing the Knight's Cross awarded on 6 October 1941 for his 42 victories. The Oak Leaves would follow ten months and exactly 60 kills later. Beerenbrock would be brought down behind enemy lines on 9 November 1942 after his machine was hit in the radiator

Taifun for Hitler's press chief, Dr Otto Dietrich, officially to announce on 9 October 1941, 'The military situation in the east has been decided. Russia is finished'. The good Doctor's words were, to say the least, a trifle premature!

On 11 October II./JG 51 was transferred down to Orel, some 200 kilometres south of the main line of advance. Here, it was to provide the fighter component of the newly established *Gefechtsverband* 'Schönborn'. This battle-group, named after Oberstleutnant Clemens *Graf* von Schönborn-Wiesentheid (the *Kommodore* of *Stukageschwader* 77, whose dive-bombers formed the group's main strike force) was engaged in the heavy fighting east of Bryansk. Before returning to the main front on 26 November, the pilots of II./JG 51 would be credited with 56 victories without loss to themselves.

In the meantime, the other *Gruppen* had not been enjoying the same level of success on the road to the Russian capital. Although an entry in a unit diary at this time surmises that the enemy was throwing in his last reserves – 'quality of pilots cannot be regarded as high-grade, as it is nearly always possible to achieve the element of surprise. Probably straight from training schools, no frontline experience, awkward and slow to make decisions' – the *Geschwader's* losses were mounting the closer they got to Moscow.

7./JG 51 were particularly hard hit. On 13 October Leutnant Joachim Hacker, who was the *Staffel's* highest scorer with 32 victories, became the latest victim of the low-level *Sturmoviks*. Taking a burst of fire when attacking a group of heavily-armoured Ilyushins, Hacker's fighter lost a wing and went straight into the ground, exploding into a fireball on impact. Nine days later 7. *Staffel's* second most successful pilot, 23-victory Oberfeldwebel Robert Fuchs, was shot down in action against a formation of high-flying DB-3 bombers.

On 23 October, future Oak Leaves winner Unteroffizier Günther Schack was forced to bale out at a height of just 100 metres after his machine was severely damaged in a dogfight. Schack was in the air again four days later as part of the *Schwarm* being led by *Staffelkapitän* Oberleutnant Herbert Wehnelt as they hunted for *Sturmoviks* above one of 2. *Panzerarmee's* armoured spearheads. Despite the appalling conditions – drizzling rain under a solid cloud base only 100 metres off the ground – they glimpsed the dim shapes of several enemy machines. But Schack's fighter was hit by German flak and he was forced to make an emergency landing.

The three remaining Messerschmitts chased after the retreating *Sturmoviks*, one of which put several rounds into Wehnelt's machine. The Bf 109 immediately went into a shallow dive, ploughing at high speed into a small wood in no-man's land. Although Wehnelt was rescued by a squad of frontline troops who had witnessed the crash, his injuries kept him off flying for almost six months. And by the time he resumed command of 7. *Staffel* on 25 April 1942, his two temporary replacements had both already been killed.

The anonymous JG 51 diarist offers some idea of the conditions being faced on the Moscow front as autumn gave way to winter;

> 28 October 1941 – Weather changing almost daily. Mostly rain and heavy cloud. Roads and airfields very boggy. Take-offs and landings only with great difficulty.
>
> 29 October 1941 – Unusually fine weather. Increased enemy air activity. Fighters and *Zementbomber* (i.e. *Sturmoviks*).
>
> 1-3 November 1941: Bad weather.
>
> 7 November 1941: Heavy snow and blizzards. Equipment unable to cope.
>
> 12 November 1941: Increased enemy activity. Temperature fallen to minus 20 degrees. Great difficulties in starting engines.

And this was only in the central sector. I. *Gruppe* faced even harsher conditions when it was sent northwards on 6 November to operate under the control of JG 54 patrolling the Lake Ilmen area of the front.

On 13 November III./JG 51 lost one of its veteran NCOs when 9. *Staffel's* Oberfeldwebel Edmund Wagner was killed in a running fight

Oberfeldwebel Edmund Wagner, pictured here (right) being congratulated by Oberstleutnant Mölders on the award of his Iron Cross, First Class, in the opening days of *Barabarossa*, was killed in action on 13 November 1941

with Soviet Pe-2 bombers. The 55-victory Wagner was honoured with a posthumous Knight's Cross four days later.

It was this same 17 November that Generaloberst Ernst Udet committed suicide in Berlin. The happy-go-lucky Udet, pre-war stunt-flyer and *bon viveur*, could no longer stand the strain of office as the Luftwaffe's head of Aircraft Procurement and Supply, particularly now that many of his peers were holding him personally responsible for the Luftwaffe's declining fortunes.

The facts of Udet's death could not be made public, of course. Instead, having lost his life 'while testing a new weapon', he was to be accorded a state funeral. This decision would have unforeseen repercussions for JG 51. Among those ordered to Berlin to form a guard of honour was the Luftwaffe's *General der Jagdflieger*, Oberst Werner Mölders.

Currently on a tour of inspection of frontline units down in the Ukraine, Mölders gladly accepted the offer of transport back to Germany in an He 111 bomber of III./KG 27 – a *Gruppe* commanded by an old friend and comrade-in-arms of *Legion Condor* days, Hauptmann Hans-Henning *Freiherr* von Beust. Piloted by Oberleutnant Kolbe, the Heinkel, with Mölders and his adjutant Major Wenzel as passengers, took off from Kherson, north of the Crimea, on 21 November. But it was destined never to reach Berlin.

The following day the He 111 was reported to be approaching Breslau flying on only one engine. Gandau airfield was covered in a heavy ground

Just eight days after the loss of Wagner, Oberst Werner Mölders, by now ***General der Jagdflieger***, prepares to depart Kherson, in the Ukraine, on 21 November for his fateful flight back to Berlin to attend Ernst Udet's state funeral. On the left is Hauptmann Hans-Henning ***Freiherr*** von Beust, ***Gruppenkommandeur*** of III./KG 27. On the right (back to camera) is Oberfeldwebel Arthur Tenz, the wireless-operator of the He 111 in the background, and one of only two of the machine's five occupants to survive the crash the following day (the other being Mölders' adjutant, Major Wenzel)

mist. Twice the pilot tried to bring the Heinkel in – unsuccessfully. As he banked away after a third failed attempt the starboard engine suddenly cut out as well. The bomber crashed on industrial land in the suburb of Schöngarten, breaking in two behind the cockpit section. Oberst Mölders, whose seat harness was unfastened, was thrown forward and killed.

On 28 November, after laying in state at the RLM, where both Hitler and Göring came to pay their respects, Mölders' coffin was borne on a gun carriage, flanked by an escort of fellow *Experten* including Adolf Galland and Karl-Gottfried Nordmann, through the streets of Berlin. Tens of thousands of mourners lined the route as the cortège slowly made its way to the Invaliden Cemetery. Here, to the sound of a salute fired by a battery of 88 mm flak guns drawn up in the nearby Tiergarten, Mölders was buried close to World War 1 hero *Rittmeister* Manfred *Freiherr* von Richthofen.

Four days prior to the funeral, on 24 November, it had been officially announced that henceforth JG 51 would bear the honour title of *Jagdgeschwader* 51 *'Mölders'*. But this had little material effect on those most immediately concerned. The harsh realities of day-to-day life on the Moscow front were too far removed from the pomp and rhetoric of Berlin. One last, all-out effort to take the Soviet capital, launched on 15 November, was already beginning to flag. A single Il-2 *Sturmovik* downed by 3./JG 51 on 19 November (the *Geschwader's* sole victory on that date) was reported to be JG 51's 1500th victory of the war.

Then, on 27 November, the temperature suddenly plummeted to 40 degrees below zero within the space of two hours. Despite this, a few ground units continued to struggle on. On the last day of the month forward patrols were just eight kilometres from the outskirts of Moscow, and 20 kilometres from the walls of the Kremlin itself!

The memorial erected by the owner of the brickworks in Breslau-Schöngarten on the exact spot beside the pond where the He 111 – '1G+BT' of 9./KG 27 – came down

Clutching his marshal's baton, Hermann Göring leads the mourners into Berlin's Invaliden Cemetery. The four helmeted figures immediately behind the *Reichsmarschall* are, from left to right, Siegfried Schnell, Josef Priller, Hans 'Assi' Hahn and Werner Streib. Among the white-lapelled Luftwaffe Generals to the rear are Hans Jeschonnek and Erhard Milch

But they could go no further. By the slenderest of margins, Hitler's great gamble – the conquest of the Soviet Union before the onset of winter – had failed. Generaloberst Heinz Guderian, whose 2. *Panzerarmee* had been stopped in its tracks at Tula by the Soviet 50th Army, admitted as much. From his HQ on the Tolstoy estate 15 kilometres south of Tula, he confided to his diary, 'The attack on Moscow has failed. We have suffered a defeat'. On 5 December the attack was called off. It was the first major reversal suffered by German ground forces since the beginning of the war. Worse was to follow.

On 6 December General Zhukov launched the ten armies of his West Front in a massive counter-offensive against Army Group Centre. Supporting this operation, the Red Air Force outnumbered the Luftwaffe 10-to-1. JG 51 was no longer strong enough to isolate the battlefield and keep the enemy at bay as it had done during the earlier 'cauldron' battles. 'Bad weather . . . 7. *Panzerdivision* pulls back 20 kilometres under heavy air attack. Own fighters unable to defend area west of Tula'.

In fact, *Führer* Directive No 39 of 8 December ordered the whole of Army Group Centre to retire to more tenable positions and dig in for the winter. But with the Moscow front effectively stalemated, Hitler had also taken the opportunity at the same time to transfer the bulk of *Luftflotte* 2 – the Air Fleet which had supported Army Group Centre since the start of *Barbarossa* – to the Mediterranean theatre for operations against Malta. Only VIII. *Fliegerkorps* was left to cover the 650-kilometre length of the central sector. And it was to this command that JG 51 was now subordinated.

On 15 December the *Geschwader* became caught up in the general withdrawal. With Soviet tanks approaching fast, the pilots of II. *Gruppe* had to vacate their base northwest of Tula in a hurry. II./JG 51's ground columns, and those of the *Stab* and IV. *Gruppe* retreating from another field some 80 kilometres distant, were covered from the air by the fighters of III./JG 51, which had only narrowly escaped encirclement in the process.

The Red Air Force did not merely enjoy numerical superiority. Its fighters were now more modern, and flown by pilots who showed 'a level of skill and courage not encountered before' – no inexperienced trainees straight from flying school these! In one dogfight between six of III./JG 51's machines and an equal number of Soviet MiG-3s, only *Gruppenkommandeur* Hauptmann Richard Leppla was able to claim a kill.

21 December saw the return of Oberstleutnant Friedrich Beckh, but the *Kommodore* was still unfit to fly operationally. It therefore fell to the *Kapitän* of 12. *Staffel*, Heinz Bär – newly promoted to hauptmann, and now fully recovered from the effects of a forced landing behind enemy lines at the end of August – to lead the *Geschwader* in the air. It was a thankless task. December's loss rate of 32 per cent was the highest suffered by JG 51 since the outbreak of war. Coupled to this was a sharp decline in the number of victories achieved. As an extreme example, Oberleutnant Helmut Lohoff's badly mauled 7. *Staffel* was credited with just four kills during the last two months of 1941.

Despite the extremely critical nature of the situation in front of Moscow, the arrival of the New Year was celebrated in traditional fashion. And, extraordinarily, some lucky pilots were still even being sent back home to Germany on leave. But then the winter-hardened Russians launched another major counter-offensive. On 4 January 1942 six Soviet armies struck along that sector of the front where the left-hand flank of Army Group Centre abutted the right wing of Army Group North.

The enemy quickly smashed a breach 100 kilometres wide. They then turned southwards towards the Rollbahn, their objective being to cut this vital supply artery and recapture the towns of Smolensk and Vyazma beyond. This would effectively isolate Army Group Centre's forces entrenched in front of Moscow. The Germans reacted furiously to this threat in their rear. The main Soviet advance was halted around the town of Rzhev, where fierce fighting would continue to rage for the remainder of January and throughout most of February.

The Rzhev region was thus to be the main area of activity for JG 51's three *Gruppen* during the first two months of 1942. II./JG 51 was the most successful, being credited with 90 enemy aircraft destroyed for the loss of just two of its own pilots (plus a third killed in a take-off accident). But the two high awards of this period both went to pilots of IV. *Gruppe* – or 12. *Staffel*, to be even more precise. Leutnant Bernd Gallowitsch received the Knight's Cross on 24 January for his 42 victories. And on 16 February, with his score standing at 90, *Staffelkapitän* Hauptmann Heinz Bär became only the second (and last) member of JG 51 to be honoured with the Swords.

Hauptmann Richard Leppla's III. *Gruppe* came a very poor third in the scoring stakes at this time, for in keeping with the close-support

Hauptmann Heinz Bär (left), sporting the Swords awarded on 16 February 1942, fails to see the funny side of whatever it is Oberfeldwebel Heinrich 'Tubby' Höfemeier is telling him

During the bitter winter of 1941-42, hangar space was at a premium. These *Friedrichs* of the *Gruppenstab* I./JG 51, jam-packed together at Staraya-Russa, are at least under cover, but the cold is still intense – note the warm-air ducting draped across the wing of the TO's machine in the foreground, and the bundled-up figures of the 'black men' . . .

role of VIII. *Fliegerkorps*, the *Geschwader's* new parent command, III./JG 51 was now being employed almost exclusively on ground-attack missions. Luckily its losses were minimal, but 7. *Staffel's* run of misfortune had not yet come to an end. Its *Kapitän*, Oberleutnant Helmut Lohoff, was brought down during a *freie Jagd* sortie near Rzhev on 11 February, and his successor, Oberleutnant Anton Niess, was reported missing after falling victim to enemy ground fire just 11 days later.

Meanwhile, just across the Army Group boundary in the northern sector, I./JG 51 continued to operate under the control of JG 54. Hauptmann Wilhelm Hachfeld's pilots had already spent Christmas completely cut off by the Red Army, but German troops had since regained the ground surrounding their base close to the southern tip of Lake Ilmen. Now this very area was to be the scene of yet a third major Soviet counter-offensive.

On 6 January five Russian armies broke through the German front south of the frozen Lake Ilmen and began to surge westwards. In so doing they encircled some 100,000 German troops around the town of Demyansk, and a further 3500 in the smaller pocket of Cholm. It was the Germans' turn to suffer the experience of being trapped in a 'cauldron'. But Hitler immediately declared the two pockets to be 'fortresses' that were to be held until relieved. In the meantime, supplies would be flown in by air.

In the coming weeks and months the primary task for I./JG 51 – together with elements of JG 54 – would be to protect the Luftwaffe's lumbering Ju 52/3m transports as they flew reinforcements, ammunition and provisions into the defenders of the two 'fortresses'. Many of the *Gruppe's* pilots increased their scores dramatically during the course of these operations. One of the first Knight's Crosses awarded in March was conferred upon Oberleutnant Heinrich Krafft, the long-serving *Kapitän* of 3. *Staffel*, for a total of 46 kills.

. . . but not all enjoyed such amenities. Here, Heinrich Krafft's 'Brown 7' pokes its nose into a makeshift servicing shed. The 47 victory bars on the rudder reveal that the *Kapitän* of 3. *Staffel* has just been awarded the Knight's Cross (for kill 46, claimed on 18 March 1942) . . .

while braving the elements out on the frozen expanse of Staraya-Russa airfield, a bearded Russian peasant drives a sledge laden with fuel – aviation spirit for I. *Gruppe's* fighters and hay for his hardy little *panje* pony

The month's three other Knight's Crosses all went to members of II./JG 51 who had distinguished themselves in the recent clashes around Rzhev. On 18 March, the day of Krafft's award, Leutnant Hans Strelow, *Kapitän* of 5./JG 51, was credited with shooting down seven enemy aircraft. This was the highest single day's total of any fighter pilot during the winter battles of 1941-42. It won Strelow an immediate Knight's Cross – for an overall score of 52 – and a mention by name in the OKW communiqué broadcast twenty-four hours later.

That same 19 March, two of the *Gruppe's* veteran NCOs, Oberfeldwebels Wilhelm Mink and Otto Tange, received their awards for 40 and 41 victories respectively. But it was Strelow's star that was in the ascendant.

On 24 March – less than a week after his Knight's Cross, but with another 16 kills already under his belt – the 20-year-old Hans Strelow

Two newly minted Knight's Cross recipients – Oberfeldwebel Otto Tange (left) and Wilhelm Mink. Neither would survive the war

became the then youngest member of the *Wehrmacht* to be honoured with the Oak Leaves.

March had witnessed some bitter fighting as the Red Army strove hard to recapture as much territory as possible before the spring thaw set in and made large-scale movement next to impossible. By contrast, the next two months remained relatively quiet as each side paused to take breath and prepare for its own forthcoming summer offensive.

April's only Knight's Cross was awarded early in the month to Oberfeldwebel Heinrich Höfemeier of I. *Gruppe* for 41 kills. Two days later, on 7 April, JG 51 recorded its 3000th victory of the war – an achievement that merited another mention for the *Jagdgeschwader 'Mölders'* in the official OKW news communiqué.

But perhaps the most significant event of the month for JG 51 was a change of command. On 10 April Oberstleutnant Friedrich Beckh departed to take up a staff position in the RLM. After *'Onkel'* Theo Osterkamp and the paternal *'Vati'* Mölders, Beckh had cut a much more distant figure. His long absence during his official tenure of office had not helped, and it is said that there were many in the *Geschwader* who did not even know who their *Kommodore* was! Beckh's replacement, Major (later Oberstleutnant) Karl-Gottfried Nordmann, hitherto the *Kommandeur* of IV. *Gruppe*, was an altogether different character. Outgoing and approachable, he had an almost photographic memory for names and faces – an invaluable asset for any commanding officer.

With the whole of III./JG 51 currently engaged almost exclusively on ground-attack operations, one of Nordmann's first acts as *Kommodore* was to relieve 2./JG 51 of the *Jabo* missions that it had been assiduously carrying out since the days of the Battle of Britain and restore the *Staffel* to a purely fighter role. This move helped to kick-start the careers of a number of future *Experten* within the *Staffel*, who until now had been unable to show their true potential. Among them were Oberfeldwebels Joachim Brendel and Josef 'Pepi' Jennewein.

But sister *Staffel* 3./JG 51 ended the month on a less happy note. On 21 April one of its pilots was killed when he crashed during his landing approach. This was the first operational fatality to be suffered by the 'Lucky Third' since its days on the Channel coast more than a year earlier!

By the first week of May 1942 land contact had been established with both the Demyansk and Cholm 'fortresses', although the former remained partially surrounded, and supplies still had to be flown in by air. I./JG 51's continuing support of these operations resulted in several casualties towards the end of the month. Among them was Leutnant Erwin Fleig, one-time wingman of Werner Mölders, whom Major Nordmann had appointed *Kapitän* of the rejuvenated 2. *Staffel* only four weeks previously. On 29 May, after claiming a MiG-3 for victory 66, Fleig's own machine was hit and he baled out over enemy territory.

Erwin Fleig, who had scored JG 51's 500th victory (a Spitfire downed on 18 September 1940) and who was a great personal friend of Werner Mölders – he had been one of the witnesses at Mölders' wedding on 13 September 1941 – was forced to bale out behind enemy lines on 29 May 1942

Two days later Hauptmann Josef Fözö, who had taken over as *Kommandeur* of I. *Gruppe* from Hauptmann Wilhelm Hachfeld on 3 May, was again seriously wounded when his *Friedrich* overturned on landing. It was the end of Fözö's operational career. After recovery, he would spend the rest of the war in various staff and training positions.

But the *Geschwader's* most grievous loss of the month had undoubtedly been that of Leutnant Hans Strelow, the *Kapitän* of 5. *Staffel*. His remarkable run of recent successes – 42 since the beginning of January alone – had come to a close with the destruction of a Pe-2 bomber to the southwest of Tula on 22 May. Strelow's fighter was damaged by return fire from the bombers, and he had had to make an emergency landing behind enemy lines. Rather than be taken prisoner by the Russian troops closing in on him, it is reported that the young Oak Leaves wearer shot himself.

By June it was clear that preparations for the *Wehrmacht's* 1942 summer offensive in the east were all but complete. But the only material reinforcement for JG 51 came in the unexpected form of a *Staffel* of Spanish volunteers. This was the second such volunteer unit that Spain's *Generalissimo* Franco had sent to Russia, the first having served originally under JG 27 during the winter of 1941-42 (see *Osprey Aviation Elite Units 12 - Jagdgeschwader 27 'Afrika'* for further details).

Attached operationally to II. *Gruppe*, the newcomers' official title was 15.(*span*)/JG 51, but Major Julio Salvador's unit was more usually referred to within the *Geschwader* simply as the '*spanische Staffel*' – the Spaniards themselves preferred *2a Escuadrilla Azul* (2nd Blue Squadron). Whatever their nomenclature, the Spaniards would fight alongside the pilots of JG 51 on the Moscow front throughout the coming summer and autumn months.

On 22 June (the day after he had welcomed the Spanish *Staffel* to his command) Major Nordmann suffered a similar accident to Josef Fözö when his machine somersaulted on landing. At first it was thought that the *Kommodore's* injuries were relatively minor, and within a few weeks he was back in the air – albeit in some pain and with impaired vision – and adding to his score. But then it was discovered that he had, in fact, suffered a fracture to the base of his skull, which was to entail a lengthy stay in hospital.

The great summer offensive was finally launched on 28 June, but it was not aimed at capturing Moscow. The *Führer* had changed his sights. The full weight of the German effort was now concentrated on the southern sector, with the twin objectives of taking Stalingrad and seizing the Russian oilfields down in the Caucasus.

In the centre, German troops would continue to defend their positions in the Vyazma bulge in front of the Soviet capital, both as a springboard for any possible future advance, but also to prevent the Red Army from counter-attacking southwards and endangering the main offensive. And for a brief period in the high summer of 1942, the *Geschwader's* scores equalled, and sometimes even surpassed, those of the heady opening days of *Barabarossa*.

II./JG 51 was particularly successful. On 5 July it were credited with 46 kills – an all-time single-day record. Acting-*Kommandeur* Hauptmann Hartmann Grasser was alone responsible for eight, with Oberleutnant Karl-Heinz Schnell, *Kapitän* of 5. *Staffel*, and Feldwebel Anton Hafner claiming six and seven respectively. This took the trio's individual totals to 61, 50 and 43. IV. *Gruppe* had its high-scorers too. In fact, the nine victories achieved by 10./JG 51's Oberfeldwebel Franz-Josef Beerenbrock on 1 August made him the *Geschwader's* highest scorer of them all to date. His total of 102 – one more than Werner Mölders' official wartime score – won him Oak Leaves two days later.

Still engaged primarily in ground-attack operations, III. *Gruppe's* modest successes were more than overshadowed by their losses. Among the casualties was *Kommandeur* Hauptmann Richard Leppla, who forced landed after being badly wounded on 2 August. Despite having lost the sight in one eye, he attempted to remain operational, only to collide with a landing Ju 52/3m when taxiing out five days later. Bowing to the inevitable, Leppla agreed to hospitalisation. He would spend much of the

10. *Staffel's* Oberfeldwebel Franz-Josef Beerenbrock often flew as *Katschmarek* (wingman) to Karl-Gottfried Nordmann during the latter's service both as *Kommandeur* of IV. *Gruppe* and, subsequently, *Geschwaderkommodore* (hence perhaps the *Geschwader-Adjutant's* insignia seen here). There appear to be exactly 100 victory bars on the machine's rudder. Two more will suffice to win Beerenbrock the Oak Leaves on 3 August 1942

When Feldwebel Anton Hafner's Knight's Cross was announced on 23 August the 'black men' of his 6. *Staffel* wasted no time in pinning a large cardboard replica of the award around his neck . . .

. . . but this is the real thing – the official photograph, albeit signed quite informally 'Toni Hafner'

remainder of the war carrying out staff and training duties, before returning to ops as *Kommodore* of JG 6 in the final weeks.

But still the *Geschwader* continued to score. 4 August saw it top the 3500 mark (the collective total by day's end being 3511). And 24 hours later a kill by 6. *Staffel's* Leutnant Herbert Puschmann gave II./JG 51 its 1000th victory of the war, making it the most successful of all the four *Gruppen*.

The growth in individual scores during this period is reflected by the higher totals amassed by the next batch of Knight's Cross winners (the first for nearly five months). The benchmark figure had been raised yet again, this time to 60 or more. On 21 August Oberleutnant Ernst Weismann of 12. *Staffel* was awarded the decoration posthumously – he had been reported missing north of Rzhev eight days earlier – for his 67 eastern front victories. 6./JG 51's Feldwebel Anton Hafner received his Knight's Cross on 23 August for a score of exactly 60. And on 4 September another NCO pilot, Oberfeldwebel Heinrich Klöpper of 11. *Staffel*, was similarly honoured for a total of 65.

By now the *Geschwader* had been strengthened by the addition of a further *Staffel* – of twin-engined Henschel Hs 129s! It had initially been the intention to equip every eastern front *Jagdgeschwader* with its own semi-autonomous *Staffel* of tank-busting Hs 129s, but JG 51 was the only *Geschwader* to actually receive them. Oberleutnant Eggers and the pilots of his *Panzerjägerstaffel* had been nearing the end of their training at Deblin-Irena, in Poland, when they were suddenly rushed forward to the Vyazma area early in August to help relieve Soviet armoured pressure on 2. and 3.*Panzerarmeen*.

While the Red Army had been concentrating all its efforts on reducing the Vyazma salient (efforts that were soon to bog down in autumnal mud),

Obtained from a JG 51 source, this shot reportedly shows an Hs 129 of the *Geschwader's* tank-busting *Staffel*, whose serviceability returns rarely reached double figures at any one time. Unfortunately, this example has broken in two just where the fuselage numeral would normally be carried, and it is thus impossible either to confirm the machine's identity or pinpoint the incident which led to its present sorry state (perhaps a ground collision with the Bf 109 just visible at background right?)

the situation beyond Army Group Centre's northern boundary had remained relatively stable. So much so, in fact, that I./JG 51 – led since Josef Fözö's accident by Hauptmann Heinrich Krafft, ex-*Kapitän* of 3. *Staffel* – was pulled out of the front at the end of August and returned to Jesau, in East Prussia, to convert on to the Focke-Wulf Fw 190.

After nearly a fortnight of retraining, and with the words of Oberstleutnant Günther Lützow ringing in their ears (now a member of *General der Jagdflieger* Adolf Galland's staff, Lützow had sped them on their way with a lengthy speech on behalf of the High Command!), I./JG 51 returned to the eastern front, thus becoming the first *Jagdgruppe* to operate the Fw 190 in Russia.

Its destination was Lyuban, southeast of Leningrad, where the *Gruppe* arrived on 10 September. Back under the control of JG 54, although sharing Lyuban with the Bf 109s of III./JG 77, Krafft's pilots would remain on the Leningrad-Volkov sector for the best part of five weeks. During this time there was little sign of activity on the part of the enemy,

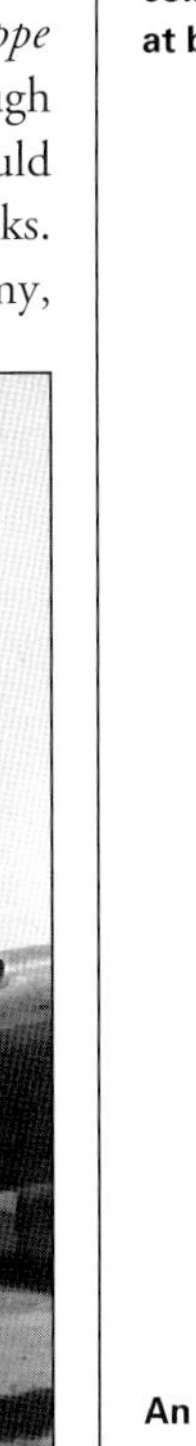

An obviously brand-new Fw 190A-3, bearing both the *Geschwader* and I. *Gruppe* badges, pictured during I./JG 51's conversion to Focke-Wulfs at Jesau, East Prussia, in September 1942

Proof that all did not go smoothly at Jesau. The Fw 190's bulky radial engine greatly obstructed forward visibility when on the ground, and made taxiing a hazardous business. If insufficient care was taken the result could be as here – the culprit is easily identified by the bent propeller blades!

and the *Gruppe* was denied the chance of really testing its new mounts. On 17 October I./JG 51 was transferred down to Vyazma finally to rejoin the rest of the *Geschwader* on the Moscow front. But even here things had by now quieted down, and for the remainder of the month the *Gruppe's* Focke-Wulfs were employed primarily in flying uneventful standing patrols over their own base.

Incidentally, in August, after recovering from his skull fracture, Karl-Gottfried Nordmann had been sent back to Germany, first on home leave and then to attend several courses. His place at the head of the *Geschwader* was filled temporarily by acting-*Kommodore* Hauptmann Joachim Müncheberg, an Oak Leaves-wearing 83-victory *Experte* who had previously commanded II./JG 26 on the Channel coast. In the two months spent in charge of JG 51 Müncheberg managed to add a further

Pictured on the eastern front – possibly at Orel – prior to withdrawal for conversion onto the Fw 190, two unteroffiziere of II./JG 51 (note the white horizontal *Gruppe* bar ahead of the black numeral) clown for the cameraman. Hermann Aubrecht, on the left, would survive the war with 31 victories. After gaining 51 kills – and the Knight's Cross – with JG 51 in Russia, Kurt Knappe (right) was posted to JG 2 in France, where he would add five more victories before being killed in action tackling RAF Spitfires on 3 September 1943

33 eastern front kills to his existing western total. The 20th of them – his 103rd overall, claimed on 9 September – had won him the Swords.

Even before I./JG 51 arrived at Vyazma with its Fw 190s, II. *Gruppe* had already been withdrawn from the front for similar re-equipment. Hauptmann Grasser's pilots flew to Jesau on 7 October, but their conversion on to the Focke-Wulf was interrupted by events elsewhere.

The campaign in Africa was not going well. On 23 October 1942 the British launched the battle of El Alamein. German intelligence had also got wind of imminent Allied landings along the coast of northwest Africa. Luftwaffe reinforcements were urgently needed in the area, and as an experienced *Jagdgruppe* not currently engaged on operations, II./JG 51 was an obvious candidate for transfer.

Consequently, Hauptmann Grasser's *Gruppenstab*, together with 4. and 5. *Staffeln*, were taken off their Focke-Wulfs and re-equipped instead with the latest Messerschmitt variant, the Bf 109G. On 8 November – the day Anglo-American forces landed in Morocco and Algeria – Hauptmann Grasser and his two *Staffeln* departed Jesau for the long haul down to Sicily, leaving just 6./JG 51 to complete its conversion on to the Fw 190.

On 1 November it had been announced that JG 51 had become the first *Jagdgeschwader* to achieve a total of 4000 enemy aircraft destroyed. Two days later 1942's last Knight's Cross went to Unteroffizier Kurt Knappe, another of II. *Gruppe's* 'old guard' NCOs, for his 51 eastern front victories to date.

But November also brought a sudden spate of losses – among them the Geschwader's highest scorer. Recently promoted to leutnant and appointed *Staffelkapitän* of 10./JG 51, Franz-Josef Beerenbrock was forced to land behind enemy lines on 9 November when his machine was hit in the radiator during a dogfight with a large gaggle of Soviet fighters. At the time of his capture, Beerenbrock's total was standing at 118.

Despite the growing numbers of enemy aircraft being encountered in the area – always a sure sign of an impending counter-offensive – III./JG 51 was withdrawn from the front on 12 November as planned and returned to Jesau for re-equipment with Focke-Wulfs. Thus, when the inevitable counter-attack came, the *Geschwader* had just two *Gruppen*, I. and IV., plus the attached Spanish and Hs 129 *Staffeln*, with which to oppose it.

The assault, launched by seven Soviet armies on 24 November, tore open Army Group Centre's left flank to the west of Rzhev. The depleted JG 51 did what it could to support the embattled ground troops, but at great cost. One of the earliest casualties was Leutnant Günther Jolas of the *Panzerjägerstaffel*, who was wounded when his Henschel was brought down by enemy ground fire.

Another pilot lost was a newcomer on his very first mission. By the end of November the Spanish volunteers, having claimed 13 victories for the loss of three of their number killed and one wounded, had completed their tour of duty and were preparing to return home. They were immediately replaced by a new *Staffel*, Major Carlos Ferrándiz's *3a Escuadrilla Azul*. Arriving from Spain via the south of France, Russia in mid-winter came as a nasty shock. 'It was horrible – I didn't think anywhere on earth could be so cold!' one groundcrew member recalled many years later. And it was the

Hauptmann Heinrich 'Gaudi' Krafft, *Gruppenkommandeur* of I./JG 51, was killed by Red Army troops after forced landing behind enemy lines southwest of Rzhev on 14 December 1942

conditions – a featureless snow-covered landscape, with the horizon obscured by thick mist and low cloud, that led to the loss of *Capitán* Andrés Asensi on the *Staffel's* first operation, flown on 1 December. It is presumed that he became disorientated and crashed behind enemy lines.

With the Soviet offensive gaining momentum, I./JG 51 had long since stopped complaining about the dearth of opponents for its new Fw 190s. On 4 December the *Gruppe* claimed a total of 27, one of which provided a first for future Knight's Cross recipient Unteroffizier Oskar Romm. Six days later a pair for Hauptmann Krafft took the *Kommandeur's* score to 78, but his wingman, Hauptmann Horst Riemann, who was also the *Gruppe's* communications officer, was shot down and killed. Four days later still, it would be Heinrich Krafft who failed to return. Brought down by Soviet anti-aircraft fire southwest of Rzhev, he was beaten to death by Russian troops.

On 17 December – the day Leutnant Rolf Kickert, Beerenbrock's recent replacement as the *Kapitän* of 10. Staffel, was lost – III./JG 51 arrived back from Jesau re-equipped with Focke-Wulfs. The absent II./JG 51's 'orphaned' 6. *Staffel* had returned some time earlier, and was now operating its Fw 190s alongside the *Geschwaderstab* as a 'special purposes' (i.e. *Jabo*) *Stabsstaffel*.

Unlike their colleagues of I. *Gruppe*, the pilots of III./JG 51 were not left to kick their heels for long. They and their new mounts were immediately thrown into the thick of the action. On his very first operation flying the Focke-Wulf, Leutnant Günther Schack claimed five Soviet Pe-2s downed and a sixth damaged.

But individual successes in the air could not halt the inexorable tide of enemy forces on the ground. By mid-December the 3rd Soviet Shock Army had surrounded some 7000 German troops at Velikiye Luki – an important road and rail junction northwest of Rzhev. Once again the *Führer* ordered the garrison to hold. Supplies were to be dropped by air (there was no landing field within the perimeter).

A special Luftwaffe *Gefechtsverband* was set up to supply the beleaguered defenders. To support this operation the Fw 190s of I./JG 51, backed up by elements of III. *Gruppe*, were pulled back from the Vyazma area to a frozen lake close to the Velikiye Luki pocket. Dubbed 'Great Ivan Lake' by the pilots, this was to be their base for the next few weeks. But despite every effort, they were unable to prevent the Soviets from overrunning Velikiye Luki. Contact with the garrison was lost on 15 January 1943.

This early Fw 190A-3 of III./JG 51, newly arrived in the Velikiye Luki area in the winter of 1942-43, is already showing distinct signs of wear and tear

Focke-Wulfs of I. *Gruppe* dispersed on the frozen surface of 'Great Ivan Lake' near Velikiye Luki in January 1943. Note the machine in the background, centre left, undergoing a complete engine change

I. *Gruppe's* Focke-Wulfs remained on their frozen 'airfield' for a further fortnight, flying *freie Jagd* sorties and escorting bomber and Stuka raids on the advancing enemy.

It was after taking off from 'Great Ivan Lake' on 17 January, and while climbing away in a tight turn, that Oberstleutnant Nordmann's Fw 190 suddenly flicked over into opposite bank (a nasty trait of the Focke-Wulf fighter when close to stalling speed) and collided with the aircraft flown by his wingman. Although Nordmann was able to bale out with nothing more than a dislocated arm, Hauptmann Rudolf Beck – who had taken command of I. *Gruppe* after the death of Heinrich Krafft just a month earlier – was killed. This incident affected Karl-Gottfried Nordmann so deeply that, although he remained *Kommodore* of JG 51 for more than year after the collision, he never flew operationally again.

On the following day (18 January) a formation of nine Pe-2 bombers attacked I./JG 51's 'Great Ivan Lake' base. Leutnant Joachim Brendel and Feldwebel Josef Jennewein happened to be in the air at the time, and in a perfect position to bounce the twin-engined Petlyakovs. It was a situation the one-time *Jabo* pilots of 2. *Staffel* had long dreamed of. Jennewein despatched five of the raiders and Brendel three – the ninth got away.

The first Knight's Cross of the year was awarded on 24 January. Like Kurt Knappe back in November, IV./JG 51's Oberfeldwebel Herbert Friebel received his decoration for 51 victories. It would appear that having risen to 60+, the yardstick for winning the Knight's Cross had now been reduced back down to the half-century mark!

On 29 January I./JG 51 transferred down to Orel on Army Group Centre's southern flank. It was replaced on 'Great Ivan Lake' by the Fw 190s of IV. *Gruppe*, which had spent the last weeks converting from *Friedrichs*. The Red Army was now pushing southwards from Velikiye

Luki, and it was over this area that Oberleutnant Wolfgang Böwing-Treuding's Focke-Wulf was brought down by ground fire on 11 February. The third *Kapitän* of 10. *Staffel* to be lost in as many months, Böwing-Treuding would be honoured with a posthumous Knight's Cross (for his final total of 46) on 24 March.

Meanwhile Soviet pressure had also been mounting along the Vyazma-Orel sector of the central front. This was reflected in JG 51's lengthening scoreboard. On 24 February I. and III. *Gruppen* between them claimed 47 enemy aircraft destroyed. Of I. *Gruppe's* 20 victories, seven had gone to 2./JG 51's 'Pepi' Jennewein and another five to his *Staffelkapitän*, Oberleutnant Edwin Thiel. Among the pair's successes was an entire formation of six *Sturmoviks*, plus their two escorting LaGG-3 fighters!

The following day the *Geschwader* was credited with a further 43 kills. But, as elsewhere, personal achievements in the air – impressive though they undoubtedly were – counted for little against the much broader backcloth of ground operations. Far to the south, 6. *Armee* had already surrendered at Stalingrad. Now, at the end of February 1943, German forces on the central sector were stretched to breaking point. On its immediate left flank, Army Group North had evacuated the long-held Demyansk pocket. III. *Gruppe* was temporarily attached to JG 54 during this period to help cover the ground troops as they pulled out.

This left the Vyazma 'bulge' in front of Moscow dangerously exposed. And after many heated arguments with his generals, the *Führer* was finally persuaded to implement Operation *'Büffel'* ('Buffalo', or 'Hard Slog') – the large-scale withdrawal from the Vyazma salient. This manoeuvre, which lasted throughout the first half of March, was supported by the Fw 190s of I. and IV. *Gruppen*. By its close, the central front had been straightened by some 230 kilometres and, as a result, 21 German divisions were freed up for deployment elsewhere. But the Vyazma 'springboard' was no more, and the constant threat it had posed to the Russian capital – however tenuous of late – had finally been lifted.

On 11 March (the day before the Soviets re-entered the town of Vyazma itself), elements of I./JG 51 moved back from Orel to Bryansk. It was from Orel, however, that 15 of the *Gruppe's* new Fw 190A-4s lifted off four days later to carry out a low-level attack on an airfield now 80 kilometres to the rear of the advancing Red Army. The airfield was on the outskirts of a little-known provincial town whose name is now enshrined in military history as the site of the greatest tank battle the world has ever seen – Kursk.

The diminutive Oberfeldwebel Josef 'Pepi' Jennewein – the 1940 slalom world ski champion – draws hungrily on a cigarette after an obviously exhausting mission

But the titanic armoured clash at Kursk was still some four months off. Early in April the spring thaw set in on the central sector. It provided a welcome respite for both sides, who were close to exhaustion after fighting each other almost to a standstill.

On 16 April the *Kapitän* of 2. *Staffel*, Oberleutnant Edwin Thiel, was awarded the Knight's Cross for the recent string of victories that had taken his total to 51. And six days later one of Thiel's most successful pilots, Leutnant Joachim Brendel, was appointed *Staffelkapitän* of 1./JG 51 after the previous incumbent, Oberleutnant Hans Boos, had been killed when he baled out during a dogfight but his parachute had failed to open.

Although the situation on the ground had stabilised, the spring and early summer of 1943 saw no let-up for JG 51's *Gruppen*. Among the many operations carried out from their bases around Orel and Bryansk were – unusually – several deep penetration missions, flown at high-altitude, and with the aid of drop tanks. Their targets were mostly Soviet

Although the undercarriage of the Fw 190 was much sturdier than that of the notoriously accident-prone Bf 109, it could only withstand so much mistreatment, as future *Experte* Unteroffizier Otto Gaiser of 10./JG 51 found out to his cost at Bryansk in March 1943. The tracks in the melting snow seem to suggest that Gaiser unwittingly taxied his 'White 10' over a bomb that someone had carelessly left lying about! Note IV. *Gruppe's* small aft fuselage cross

The Focke-Wulf's wide-legged stance proved its worth during the spring thaw of 1943. This I. *Gruppe* machine, with 'Pepi' Jennewein at the controls, ploughs its way almost hub-deep across a waterlogged field, throwing up mud and muck as it goes

lines of communication and troop concentrations inside the huge salient which the Red Army's recent advances had punched through the German front around Kursk.

The Fw 190 pilots also escorted a number of bomber and Stuka raids over the same area. During one such operation, which saw 60 dive-bombers target Kursk station on 22 May, I./JG 51 became embroiled with a large group of Russian-flown Airacobras. 2. *Staffel's* Oberfeldwebel Jennewein added a brace of the lend-lease machines to a total that already topped the 60 mark. On the other side of the coin, another of 2./JG 51's high-scoring Oberfeldwebeln, 54-victory Heinz Leber, fell victim to anti-aircraft fire northeast of Orel on 1 June.

The following day the *Geschwader* reported its 5000th victory. By this time the Luftwaffe airfields in the Orel-Bryansk region were beginning to fill up with aircraft being brought into the area in preparation for the forthcoming German offensive aimed at eliminating the Kursk 'bulge'. JG 51's fighters were also tasked with protecting these inviting targets against attack from the Red Air Force. One report claims that the Focke-Wulfs destroyed 51 enemy machines without loss on 8 June!

On 22 June there was a change of command at the head of III. *Gruppe* when Hauptmann Karl-Heinz Schnell – who had often led the *Geschwader* in the air since Nordmann's accident at the beginning of the year – was appointed to a position within the RLM. It was suggested tongue-in-cheek that Schnell's superiors, many of whom he had criticised in the past for their conduct of operations, wanted to keep a closer eye on him! 'Bubi' Schnell had been a member of the *Geschwader* since the pre-war days of I./JG 71. His replacement, a complete newcomer, was an equally outspoken character.

Ground collisions were an ever-present danger on overcrowded landing fields. With its operational days over, 3./JG 51's 'Brown 3' is plundered for spare parts. While one mechanic wrestles with the cockpit instrument panel, another is clearly intent on retrieving something useable from the stricken fighter's radio compartment . . .

Hauptmann Fritz Losigkeit's operational career to date had included spells both in a Spanish Republican gaol (after being shot down during the Civil War) and as Air Attaché in Tokyo (whence he had returned aboard a blockade runner). In between times, he had served on the Channel coast, in Defence of the Reich and on the Russian front – latterly as *Kommandeur* of I./JG 26. He thus brought with him to III./JG 51 a wealth of experience, but just seven kills.

At the end of June the third Spanish *Staffel's* tour of duty in Russia expired. Their seven months on the eastern front had netted the Spaniards a respectable 62 victories against a loss of six of their own. They were in turn succeeded by a *4a Escuadrilla Azul*. The newcomers, commanded by Major Mariano Cuadra, did not take up station alongside JG 51 in the Orel area immediately, however, but were instead deployed some way to the rear on a field to the southeast of Smolensk. The reasons for this were twofold – their inexperience, and the fact that their arrival coincided to the day with the launch of Operation *Zitadelle*.

Compared to Hitler's previous summer offensives in the east – *Barbarossa* in 1941, which had failed to capture Moscow, and *Blau/Braunschweig* in 1942, which had not succeeded in taking either Stalingrad or the Caucasian oilfields – the aims of *Zitadelle* were more modest. The *Führer's* intention was first to pinch off the 'bulge' in the German front created by the Red Army's advance westward past Kursk, and then systematically to destroy the Soviet forces that were trapped inside it.

Some have likened the 1943 offensive to little more than a 'tidying up' of the frontline, but this is not altogether fair. The Kursk salient, measuring some 200 kilometres from north to south, covered a huge area

. . . sister ship 'Brown 2' is far less seriously damaged. It has simply nosed over in the soft ground just inches away from the steel mesh surface of its dispersal point. This rather undignified pose was known in Luftwaffe circles as a *Fliegerdenkmal*, or 'airman's monument' . . .

. . . while 'Brown 1' has obviously forced-landed away from base. It too is recoverable, however, and may well be the same 'Brown 1' in which 3. *Staffel's* Unteroffizier Fritz Haese was subsequently shot down and killed southeast of Orel on 26 July 1943

of ground. Straddling the boundary between Army Groups Centre and South, it was shaped like a giant clenched fist pushing deep into German territory. It contained 11 Soviet armies, and if these were lost, it would represent a major defeat for the Russians.

The German plan called for simultaneous offensives to be mounted from both the northern and southern shoulders of the salient. These would then meet in the middle, near the town of Kursk itself, effectively trapping those Red Army units within the 'bulge'. And although Kursk is now rightly remembered as the world's largest ever tank battle, nearly 5000 aircraft of the two opposing air forces repeatedly clashed in the clear skies overhead.

From their bases around Orel and Bryansk, the 123 Focke-Wulfs of JG 51's *Stab* and three *Gruppen* formed the main fighter component of the northern strike force.

For most of the *Geschwader's* pilots Operation *Zitadelle* began at 0300 hrs on the morning of 5 July when they took off to escort formations of Ju 87s and Ju 88s sent to blast a path through the enemy's frontline

With the earth beneath the wheels of his Focke-Wulf baked hard by the Russian summer sun, a pilot obeys his mechanic's hand signals as he taxies back in after another successful mission

defences. A few had already been aloft for 30 minutes, the first of the unbroken – and largely uneventful – succession of standing patrols over their own airfields which would continue until 2100 hrs.

The first serious fighter confrontations did not take place until the afternoon. These gave JG 51's new generation of *Experten*, the likes of Joachim Brendel and Josef Jennewein, ample opportunity to add to their growing scores. But one name eclipsed all others during the opening rounds at Kursk.

Since joining the *Geschwader* late in 1941, 8. *Staffel's* Oberfeldwebel Hubert Strassl had been credited with 37 victories. In the first four days of *Zitadelle* he would nearly double that figure. In four separate sorties to the south of Orel during the afternoon and evening of 5 July, he claimed 15 enemy aircraft destroyed. The following day he added another ten, for which he was nominated for the Knight's Cross.

On 7 July, very near to exhaustion, Strassl was able to down just two. Twenty-four hours later it was three more, but then Strassl himself was caught at low-level by a group of four LaGG-3s. As he tried to gain height, a burst from one of the Lavochkins shredded the wing of his 'Black 4'. Strassl baled out, but at 300 metres, he was too low for his parachute to open properly.

Oberfeldwebel Strassl had been only the fourth *Zitadelle* fatality for JG 51. But on the fifth day of the offensive the enemy's local air superiority began to make itself felt. Luftwaffe pilots were also somewhat disconcerted to discover that the Red Air Force had abandoned its usual untidy gaggles and was starting to adopt German tactics. The four LaGGs that had brought down Strassl's Focke-Wulf had been flying in perfect *Schwarm* formation.

On 11 July IV./JG 51 lost its *Kommandeur* when Major Rudolf Resch was shot down. Resch, who had taken over the *Gruppe* back in March, had won the Knight's Cross as a member of JG 52 in September 1942. He was just six short of his century at the time of his death. The *Kapitän* of his 12. *Staffel*, future *Sturm-Experte* Hauptmann Wilhelm Moritz, was appointed acting-*Kommandeur* in his stead until a permanent replacement could be brought in.

By this time Army Group Centre's southward push down into the Kursk salient had already stalled. Then, on 12 July, the Soviets counter-attacked in the Army Group's rear to the north of Orel. This 270-kilometre-long sector of the front thinly held by *2. Panzerarmee* was ripped open in three places.

Alarmed by this sudden threat, dissatisfied with the progress being made against the 'bulge' – German forces had so far covered less than a quarter of the distance separating its northern and southern shoulders – and unnerved by the Anglo-American landings in Sicily two days earlier (which would demand large-scale troop withdrawals from the eastern front to the Mediterranean area), Hitler called off *Zitadelle* on 13 July.

It was the turning point of the war in the east. Although it had lasted little more than a week, the *Führer's* third summer offensive would prove to be an even greater disaster than either of the other two. As the German divisions began to pull back from the Kursk perimeter, the Red Army was hot on their heels. And there it would remain until Russian troops reached the centre of Berlin 21 months later.

Oberfeldwebel Hubert Strassl of 8./JG 51, who would be honoured with a posthumous Knight's Cross for his incredible string of victories during the opening days of *Zitadelle* before he was himself killed in action south of Ponyri on 8 July 1943

II. *GRUPPE* 1942-44

After their planned conversion to Fw 190s at Jesau in East Prussia had been called off, the pilots of Hauptmann Hartmann Grasser's II./JG 51 – minus 6. *Staffel* – had immediately been despatched to the Messerschmitt assembly plants at Leipzig and Wiener Neustadt to collect a full complement of new tropicalised Bf 109G-2s. They then flew south, via Italy and Sicily, to Tunisia, in North Africa. They arrived at Sidi Ahmed, near Bizerta, on 14 November 1942. Here, they were placed under the local air command, *Fliegerführer Tunis*.

Having 'exchanged the lice of Russia for the flies of Africa', the newcomers were allowed a whole day to acclimatise themselves to their new surroundings. They were given a series of lectures on such subjects as the types of Allied aircraft they were most likely to encounter, action to be taken after a forced landing in the desert, ditching and baling out over water, and much more. Their tasks were also spelled out – *freie Jagd* and ground-attack escort missions over the fighting fronts, guarding the sea and air supply routes across the Mediterranean and protecting the ports and airfields of entry. Then they were on their own.

Their first day of operations, 16 November, resulted in a single Spitfire victory for 4. *Staffel's* Feldwebel Anton Hafner. He was again among the claimants the following day, as was Hauptmann Grasser, when British bombers attacked the *Gruppe's* Sidi Ahmed base and four were brought down. Identified at the time as Beauforts, these were in fact Blenheim Vs of No 18 Sqn.

The large white numeral and lack of a II. *Gruppe* bar indicate this Bf 109G-2/trop to be a machine of 3./JG 1 recently arrived in Tunisia. The details in this photograph, possibly taken at Bizerta, should inspire diorama fans – note the cannibalised remains of a pressurised Bf 109G-1 (of 11./JG 2?) to the right, and the Ju 52/3m that has come to grief in the background. Three more Ju 52/3m transports can also be seen on final approach

On 25 November another unit was added to *Fliegerführer Tunis'* order of battle. One of three separate high-altitude *Staffeln* sent to Tunisia, 3./JG 1 had previously served on the north German coast in defence of the Reich, before exchanging its pressurised Bf 109G-1s for G-2/trops and staging southwards. After its arrival in North Africa Oberleutnant Hans Heidrich's *Staffel* was incorporated into II. *Gruppe* as the new 6./JG 51. This occasion was unhappily marked by the loss of one of its NCO pilots, who was shot down by Spitfires southwest of Tunis – II./JG 51's first fatality in the Mediterranean theatre.

The following day (27 November), the other two *Staffeln* more than redressed the balance by claiming seven Spitfires in the Tunis area. The seemingly unstoppable 'Toni' Hafner got two, whilst among the others credited were the *Kommandeur* and two of the *Gruppe's* up-and-coming *Experten*, Hauptmann Günther Rübell and Oberleutnant Karl Rammelt. The latter added another brace of Spitfires to his score 24 hours later, while Feldwebel Anton Hafner claimed JG 51's first ever American victim – the earlier aircraft recognition lecture was perhaps not as thorough as it might have been, as Hafner reported the US Flying Fortress as a Short Stirling!

The first week of December saw II./JG 51 take a steady toll of British and American fighters – some two dozen in all – without loss. A spell of exceptionally wet weather curtailed operations in mid-month, but once the action picked up again, Anton Hafner added to his score almost every time the *Gruppe* was scrambled.

But 18 December was to prove slightly out of the ordinary. On that date – when Leutnant Alfred Rauch, who was to be one of the *Geschwader's* last Knight's Cross recipients, also misidentified the B-17 he had destroyed as another Stirling – Feldwebel Anton Hafner was credited with two of the bombers' P-38 escorts. He later met and chatted to one of the downed

Proving that Tunisia was not all sun and sand, 6./JG 51's 'Yellow 5' is towed across a roadway in decidedly wet and windy conditions. While a tractor – just visible beyond the starboard wingtip – is doing most of the work, a groundcrewman struggles to heave the tail unit around to the left

A thoroughly disgruntled 1Lt N L Widen of the USAAF's 1st Fighter Group stands surrounded by curious II./JG 51 personnel after his P-38 was shot down by Feldwebel Anton Hafner (left) on 18 December 1942. After the war Norman Widen went to Germany, where he was presented with the items 'Toni' Hafner had left to him in his will – his officer's dagger and his German Cross in Gold (awarded to Hafner on 22 May 1942). Widen's blackened eyes, incidentally, are not a sign of maltreatment, but an application of burnt cork used to reduce the sun's glare – a trick quickly adopted by a number of II./JG 51's pilots!

Lightning pilots, 1Lt N L Widen. For some reason, this event made such a lasting impression on 'Toni' Hafner that he went so far as to remember his opponent in his will! After the war the then Maj Norman Widen was invited to Germany by Hafner's brother Alfons to receive his 'legacy'.

Up until now, with over 50 victories gained at a cost of just two pilots killed and four wounded, things had been going very much II./JG 51's way. But, as in Russia, the enemy's superiority in numbers was beginning to make itself felt. In January 1943 alone the *Gruppe* would suffer eight casualties, and the first of them was Feldwebel Anton Hafner.

He had already claimed one P-38 on 2 January when, later that same afternoon, the Bf 109G-2s of II./JG 51 became involved in a dogfight with two squadrons of Spitfires over Pont du Fahs. Hafner's machine was hit and he was wounded. In baling out he received further injuries as the aircraft began to break up. Although quickly rescued and taken to a field dressing station, Hafner's African war – 20 kills in seven weeks – was over. On 3 January he was put aboard an Me 323 for the flight back across the Mediterranean to a base hospital in Naples. And from there he would be returned to Germany to spend the next six months undergoing treatment.

By the second week in February the ever-increasing tempo of operations had reduced the *Gruppe's* serviceability figures to zero, so the pilots returned to Sicily to collect new Bf 109G-4s and -6s. A small *Kommando*, led by Unteroffizier Willi Schenk, was then deployed to Sardinia to reinforce the Italian fighter units defending that island's airfields and docks from American bombing attacks. During one such raid on 28 February Schenk's Bf 109G-4 was shot down in combat with '60 fighters' of the bombers' escort force. He parachuted into the sea south of Sardinia, but drowned before he could be rescued.

The bulk of the *Gruppe* was already back in Tunisia by then, but there had been no let-up in Allied pressure. By 3 March just six of the new

Gustavs remained serviceable. Further machines had to be ferried in from Sicily, but the only ones available were G-2s. The rest of the month was mainly spent in costly ground-attack missions in southern Tunisia, where the British 8th Army was about to outflank the frontier defences of the Mareth Line. By month's end II./JG 51 had lost six more pilots, and its serviceability returns were back down into single figures. Yet more aircraft had to be brought in, and this time the *Gruppe* got G-4s.

In the midst of all these depredations, on 14 March, the award of two Knight's Crosses was announced – Günther Rübell and the long-serving Oberfeldwebel Otto Schultz of 4. *Staffel* received their decorations for 43 and 51 victories respectively. On 25 March Hauptmann Hartmann Grasser's 11th North African victory took his total to 103 – more than enough for the Oak Leaves at that time. But Grasser would have to wait more than five months before getting his award. And by then he had long relinquished command of the *Gruppe*, been promoted to major and taken up a staff position.

The end in Tunisia was now approaching fast. Although some pilots – most notably Oberleutnant Karl Rammelt, the newly appointed *Kapitän* of 4. *Staffel* – continued to claim successes into April, II./JG 51, like all Axis forces in the country, was being pushed back towards the shrinking perimeter around the capital, Tunis. On 8 April it moved to Menzel Temime, an airfield on the east coast of the Cape Bon peninsula, where its personnel began to prepare for evacuation.

On 11 April the first groundcrews left by air for Trapani in Sicily, but two of their Ju 52/3ms were shot down by Allied fighters off the coast. One week later the *Gruppe* flew its final operations from African soil. The following day, 19 April, it passed the last of its G-4s over to JG 77, receiving a handful of the latter's war-weary G-2s in exchange. That same evening most pilots took off for San Pietro, in Sicily, where they landed by the light of burning oil drums placed at intervals along the runway.

Pilots of 4./JG 51 in a *Kübelwagen* runabout. At the wheel is Günther Stedtfeld, with future Knight's Cross recipient Otto Schultz in the seat behind him. Both would survive the war, with 32 and 73 victories respectively – all scored with JG 51

II./JG 51's Tunisian odyssey was at an end. It had claimed 121 Allied aircraft destroyed, but at a cost of 26 pilots killed, missing or wounded. With the latter figure being just two short of the *Gruppe's* official establishment of pilots upon its arrival in Africa five months earlier, this total represented an almost 100 per cent loss rate.

May and June 1943 would be spent shuttling between airfields in Sicily and Sardinia. On 7 June Oberleutnant Karl Rammelt, who had been leading the *Gruppe* since Hartmann Grasser's departure in April, was officially appointed *Kommandeur*. Although II./JG 51 was brought back up to strength by several intakes of freshly-trained young pilots during this period, the increasingly heavy Allied bombing raids on the Luftwaffe's known bases in the area caused substantial material damage.

On 10 July Anglo-American forces invaded Sicily and II./JG 51 was immediately transferred in to Trapani on the northwestern tip of the island. From here it flew three missions on the opening day of the invasion, and nine on each of the two succeeding days. Although these operations were mainly ground-strafing sorties against enemy troop movements, the *Gruppe* nonetheless managed to claim 26 aerial kills – four of them were

II./JG 51 under Allied bomb attack, probably in Sicily, circa June 1943

Hauptmann Günther Rübell is seen here sporting the Knight's Cross he won as an oberleutnant and *Kapitän* of 5. *Staffel* on 4 March 1943 for 43 victories

credited to Karl Rammelt. But seven of its own number were shot down and killed, all of them from the ranks of the recent replacements.

By this time the *Gruppe* had been bombed out of Trapani, and the individual *Staffeln* were dispersed on smaller landing strips in the surrounding countryside. But, as in Tunisia, II./JG 51 would be spared the last stages of the Sicilian campaign. On 13 July they it orders to evacuate the island. All serviceable aircraft were blown up, and remaining personnel retired to an airfield near Brindisi, on the heel of Italy. From here they were then sent to Treviso, in northern Italy, to re-equip. Before they could do so, however, fresh instructions arrived – they were to return to Germany and retrain as a specialist anti-bomber unit. The *Gruppe* arrived at Munich-Neubiberg on 18 August.

A number of Hauptmann Rammelt's surviving *'alte Hasen'* ('old hares', or veterans) had been able to claim heavy bombers during the Tunisian campaign, but these had been brought down in small-scale actions. It was an entirely different story in Defence of the Reich, where the British-based US Eighth Air Force was now sending formations of bombers several hundred-strong against German targets.

The *Kommandeur* therefore insisted on a thorough training programme to prepare his pilots for the task ahead. They practised formation attacks in *Gruppe* and *Staffel* strength, with Luftwaffe bombers playing the role of the enemy – until one trainee misjudged his approach and collided head-on with an He 111. Even more traumatic perhaps was a visit to Neubiberg some days later by Luftwaffe C-in-C *Reichsmarschall* Hermann Göring, who welcomed Rammelt's assembled pilots to Defence of the Reich operations with a speech that was not exactly effusive (see *Osprey Aircraft of the Aces 68 - Bf 109 Defence of the Reich Aces* for further details).

II./JG 51's initiation into homeland defence proper came on 14 October 1943 when the Eighth Air Force mounted its second major attack on the ball-bearing works at Schweinfurt. Taking off at 1300 hrs, Hauptmann Rammelt led the *Gruppe* northwestwards in tight formation. They sighted American B-17s north of Frankfurt 80 minutes later. In the action that followed Rammelt's pilots were credited with nine bombers destroyed. Among those claiming were the *Kommandeur* himself (his 30th) and the *Kapitän* of 5. *Staffel*, Oberleutnant Günther Rübell (48th). Their only casualty was one pilot slightly wounded, but they lost five of their new G-6s, with four pilots – including Rammelt – baling out and the fifth making a forced landing.

On 2 November the *Gruppe* faced another major incursion. This time it was a mixed force of B-17s and B-24s of the newly established Fifteenth Air Force, flying up from the Mediterranean to attack the Bf 109 works at Wiener-Neustadt. Misdirected at first towards Innsbruck, II./JG 51 did not engage the bombers until after they had carried out their attack. But it then hacked two Flying Fortresses and three Liberators from the enemy formations as they retired southwards. Again, losses amounted to one pilot wounded and five *Gustavs* downed.

The following month II./JG 51 was transferred to the Udine region of northeastern Italy. From here it was to provide the first line of defence against the Fifteenth Air Force's bombers heading up across the Alps towards targets in Austria and southern Germany. But on Christmas Day 1943, Udine itself was one of the targets for the Fifteenth's 'heavies'.

This Bf 109G-6/trop of II./JG 51 carries no identifying markings other than the *Geschwader* badge ahead of the filter on the supercharger air intake. It was photographed 'somewhere in the Mediterranean' in the late summer of 1943

The *Gruppe* did not claim any bombers, but after a running dogfight with their escorts, its pilots were credited with six P-38s without loss.

Three days later II./JG 51 was responsible for four of the ten 376th BG Liberators shot down during a raid on the marshalling yards at Vincenza. It cost the *Gruppe* two wounded, one of whom was Hauptmann Karl Rammelt – he had managed to jettison his damaged canopy and bale out at the very last moment. Oberleutnant Günther Rübell would command the *Gruppe* in his stead for the next few weeks.

Early in the new year it was thus Rübell who led II./JG 51 down to the airfield near Rome that was to be its base for operations over the Monte Cassino sector of the Italian front. But after Allied troops landed at Anzio, 45 kilometres to the south of the Italian capital, on 22 January 1944, it was here that the *Gruppe* was next employed. Their anti-bomber role temporarily in abeyance, pilots flew instead mainly as cover for the

5. *Staffel's* Oberfeldwebel Wilhelm Mink, who was severely wounded in action against B-26 Marauders northwest of Rome on 3 February 1944. The lack of a *Geschwader* badge on this G-6/trop 'gunboat' and the small 'White 12' individual aircraft number partially visible above the wing leading-edge would seem to suggest that this machine belongs to the Italian-based JG 77

Luftwaffe's ground-assault aircraft during their near-suicidal attacks on the Allied invasion beaches and offshore shipping.

Yet, it was in action against bombers that the *Kapitän* of 6. *Staffel* was to lose his life. After engaging a formation of 30 B-26 Marauders northwest of Rome on 3 February, Hauptmann Herbert Puschmann's G-6 was last seen going down out of control into thick cloud. The 54-victory Puschmann – whose place at the head of 6./JG 51 was taken by Oberleutnant Otto Schultz – would receive a posthumous Knight's Cross on 5 April.

The same formation of B-26 mediums also brought to an end the operational career of Knight's Cross holder Oberfeldwebel Wilhelm Mink of 5./JG 51. The severely wounded Mink would, after recovery, spend the rest of his war as a fighter instructor. He was killed over Denmark on 12 March 1945 when the Fw 58 courier machine he was piloting was shot down by RAF fighters.

By the end of March II./JG 51 was on the move again. This time its course took it eastwards across the Adriatic to Nis, in Yugoslavia. And it was here, in the Balkans and southeast Europe, that the *Gruppe* would remain until its disbandment 12 months hence.

April and May 1944 saw a succession of transfers as II./JG 51 was shuttled back and forth between airfields in Yugoslavia, Rumania and Bulgaria. As a dedicated anti-bomber unit, the *Gruppe's* primary task in the coming weeks would be to help defend the vitally important Rumanian oilfields around Ploesti, which were now within the range of both the Fifteenth Air Force in Italy to the southwest, and the Red Air Force fast advancing from the east.

Since the historic raid by Libyan-based Liberators of the USAAF on 1 August 1943, the Ploesti fields had received little attention. All that was to change early in April 1944, when the Fifteenth Air Force began a

No doubt about this *Gustav's* parent unit. Photographed in the Balkans in the summer of 1944, 4. *Staffel's* 'White 7', the mount of Leutnant Elias Kühlein, displays a copybook set of II. *Gruppe* markings, plus a formation leader's white rudder and the pilot's own elaborate 'eye' motif on the '*Beule*' (machine gun breech fairing)

sustained offensive (albeit aimed initially not at the oilfields and refining facilities themselves, but at the local marshalling yards, with the objective of disrupting fuel supplies to the Axis fighting fronts). In the first such attack, on 5 April, II./JG 51's *Gustavs* claimed six B-24s without loss.

After a brief diversion late in May to support Operation *Rösselsprung* ('Knight's move') – an attempt by German paratroops to capture Yugoslavia's Marshal Tito in his partisan HQ, high in the mountains of Bosnia – II./JG 51 returned to the defence of Ploesti. It was credited with six B-17s downed during the US raid of 23 June, and five Liberators in the next attack 24 hours later. But its most successful day spent protecting Rumania's oil came on 15 July, when pilots managed to claim seven B-24s – again without loss – out of the force of more than 600 'heavies' sent against the Ploesti refineries.

By this time 5./JG 51 had been detached from the rest of the *Gruppe* and transferred down to the Aegean. Based first at Kalamaki, in Greece, and then on the island of Crete (with a small *Kommando* also deployed on Rhodes), the *Staffel's* job was to provide fighter cover for the ships and transport aircraft supplying the German garrisons on the outlying Aegean islands. Just how thinly stretched II./JG 51 had become, and how diverse its responsibilities now were, may be judged from the fact that on 20 July – the day Leutnant Götz Bergmann the leader of the Rhodes *Kommando,* lost his life in a take-off accident – a pilot of the *Gruppenstab* was shot down by Mustangs while escorting ground-assault aircraft attacking partisans in Montenegro.

The following month witnessed some fundamental changes. The Luftwaffe High Command had decreed that all *Jagdgruppen* should be increased in strength from three component *Staffeln* to four. II./JG 51 underwent reorganisation accordingly, an on 15 August 4./JG 51 became 7./JG 51, and a new 8. *Staffel* was added to the *Gruppe's* establishment.

Then, nine days later, the whole southeastern theatre was thrown into turmoil by Rumania's capitulation and subsequent declaration of war against Germany. After an abortive attempt to retreat into a state of neutrality, Bulgaria followed suit on 8 September.

Based near the Bulgarian capital Sofia on the day Rumanian forces laid down their arms, the bulk of the *Gruppe's Gustavs* were immediately sent up to Ploesti to help secure the oilfields. But when Rumania actively changed sides on 25 August, their position became untenable and they retired northwards into Hungary, having lost one 7. *Staffel* pilot, possibly to Rumanian anti-aircraft fire. From Nis, in Yugoslavia, 6./JG 51 flew a few last sorties against their erstwhile allies, ground-strafing Rumanian airfields and – according to some sources – engaging Rumanian-flown Bf 109s. The *Staffel* was then also deployed temporarily down to Greece, this time to provide cover for the German withdrawal.

By 2 September II./JG 51 had taken up residence at Budak, southwest of the Hungarian capital Budapest. Its strength returns for that date indicate that the *Gruppe* possessed eight fighters, just two of which were serviceable! After fresh intakes of men and machines during the course of the month, it would be fully operational again by October. And although still not reunited with the main body of the *Geschwader* from which it had been separated in November 1942, it was now about to play its own small part in the final act of the eastern front drama.

DEFEAT IN THE EAST 1943-45

The abandonment of *Zitadelle* and withdrawal from the Kursk perimeter had set in motion a general German retreat that was to be bitter, prolonged and, ultimately, to no avail. For JG 51's eastern front *Gruppen* it would mean retracing their steps back along the line of the Moscow-Minsk Rollbahn and beyond, across Poland, past Warsaw, into Germany and right up to the gates of Berlin.

In the immediate aftermath of *Zitadelle* the *Geschwader* still had some 60 machines serviceable. On 27 July 1943 it was announced that the *Geschwader* had achieved its 6000th victory. But the closing stages of the conflict in the east were to develop primarily into a war of attrition. And in any such contest there could be only one winner – the Soviet Union, with its enormous industrial capacity deep in the Russian hinterland, untouched by Luftwaffe bombs, and supplemented by vast amounts of lend-lease material supplied by the United States.

German industry performed prodigious feats in trying to match the enemy's output, but the first cracks were already beginning to appear. Fw 190 production could no longer meet the pressing demands of both the fighter and ground-attack arms, so at the end of July 1943, IV./JG 51 – commanded now by Hauptmann Hans-Ekkehard Bob, hitherto the *Staffelkapitän* of 9./JG 54 – was ordered to relinquish its Focke-Wulfs and convert back onto Bf 109G-6s.

The Luftwaffe's training establishments were also at full stretch, and they too were facing problems. Although they could still make good the numerical losses, the newly qualified trainees they were sending to the front naturally lacked the operational experience of many of those they were replacing. The newcomers were thus much more likely to fall victim to the enemy's growing numbers. And when they did, those that in turn replaced them – who were themselves the products of increasingly rudimentary training programmes (the schools were the first to feel the effects of the looming fuel crisis) – were even more vulnerable.

And although it was the now all-but forgotten names of these replacements that were to dominate JG 51's casualty lists during the closing stages of the war – the *Geschwader* would suffer close on 300 pilots killed or missing post-*Zitadelle* – it was the steady trickle of losses among the long-serving formation leaders, *Staffelkapitäne* and *Schwarmführer*, and the higher scoring *Experten,* that would be the hardest to make good.

Three such casualties were incurred in the weeks immediately following the withdrawal from Kursk. On 26 July the 86-victory Oberfeldwebel Josef 'Pepi' Jennewein of 2./JG 51 was reported missing after being brought down behind enemy lines east of Orel. Four days later Leutnant Otto Tange of the *Stabsstaffel* suffered a direct flak hit and his 'Black 4' crashed burning into a Russian village. And on 7 August Leutnant

Two of the *Experten* lost in the immediate aftermath of *Zitadelle* – Oberfeldwebel Josef Jennewein who, although shown here in front of 2. *Staffel's* 'Black 5', was in fact flying 'Black 7' when reported missing east of Orel on 26 July 1943 . . .

. . . and Leutnant Otto Tange of the *Stabsstaffel* (pictured here as an oberfeldwebel), whose 'Black 4' took a direct flak hit on 30 August 1943

Heinrich Höfemeier of 3./JG 51 was also shot down by Soviet anti-aircraft fire. Like Tange, Höfemeier had been awarded the Knight's Cross back in the spring of 1942. Since then their scores had risen to 68 and 96 respectively.

By early August the *Geschwader* had been driven from its bases around Orel and had transferred northwest to Bryansk. Later in the month would come a parting of the ways when individual *Gruppen* were despatched from one fresh point of danger to the next as Soviet pressure mounted all along the frontline from the Baltic to the Black Sea. For by now, excluding JG 5 up in the Arctic, there were just three *Jagdgeschwader* facing the Russians – JG 54 on the northern sector (see *Osprey Aviation Elite Units 6 - Jagdgeschwader* 54 *'Grünherz'* for further details), JG 52 on the southern (see *Osprey Aviation Elite Units 16 - Jagdgeschwader* 52 for further details) and JG 51 in the centre.

Such an arrangement may have looked all very neat and tidy on the situation maps back at rear-area HQs, but the reality at the front was very different. No one *Geschwader* was strong enough to counter an all-out enemy offensive in its own particular sector. Help had to be rushed in from neighbouring areas in what came to be known as 'fire-brigade actions'.

In the second week of August 1943, for example, while III./JG 51 remained to protect the Rollbahn around Smolensk, I. and IV. *Gruppen* were hurriedly sent south to landing strips near Poltava, in the Ukraine, where the Red Army was about to recapture the important city of Kharkov. Both *Gruppen* became heavily involved in the air operations

Aircraft losses were mounting too. Although the unknown pilot no doubt survived this neatly executed belly-landing near Czemlysh in August, 7. *Staffel's* 'White 6' has split open aft of the cockpit and now lies broken-backed – a total write-off

around this major transport and industrial centre which was the key to the whole southern sector (the city had already changed hands three times).

At the end of the month, leaving IV. *Gruppe's* Bf 109s to continue supporting JG 52 in the south, Major Erich Leie's I./JG 51 was recalled to the Smolensk area, where fresh fighting had flared up. The intensity of the air war on both central and southern sectors during this period may be gauged from the fact that the *Geschwader* recorded its 7000th victory on 15 September. But the Red Army was unstoppable. Kharkov had finally been retaken on 23 August, Poltava fell exactly one month later and on 25 September the Russians liberated Smolensk. And so it would go on.

On 18 October the Hs 129s of Pz.J.St./JG 51, which had been principally engaged on the southern sector, left the *Geschwader* to become part of a new all-Henschel ground-assault *Gruppe*. From now until its eventual disbandment in April 1945, the *Staffel* would operate as 14.(Pz)/SG 9. October also saw the first Knight's Cross to be awarded for more than six months. Günther Schack had joined JG 51 as a gefreiter back in the spring of 1941. It had taken him over two years to amass his first 50 eastern front victories, but he had then been credited with 40 kills in August's recent fierce fighting alone. And on 29 October the now Leutnant Günther Schack finally received the Knight's Cross for an unprecedented 116(!) enemy aircraft destroyed.

Meanwhile, Soviet momentum in the south continued unabated. On 6 November the Red Army recaptured Kiev, the capital of the Ukraine. This left no natural barriers or major conurbations between the Soviets and the Polish border now only some 180 kilometres to the west. Having returned briefly to the central sector, IV./JG 51's *Gustavs* were rushed back southwards, only to get caught up in the general retreat. When the Russians broke out of their Kiev bridgehead in December, the *Gruppe* just managed to escape from its base near Zhitomir at the very last moment. Hauptmann Adolf Borchers' 11. *Staffel* took off as the first Soviet tank shells were exploding on the runway.

The final two months of 1943 brought a spate of Knight's Crosses. On 12 November Oberleutnant Karl-Heinz Weber, the *Kapitän* of 7. *Staffel*, received his for exactly 100 victories. On the same day Oberfeldwebel Hubert Strassl was honoured posthumously for his incredible run of successes during the opening stages of *Zitadelle*. Two more awards were made on 22 November, both to *Staffelkapitäne* – 1./JG 51's Oberleutnant Joachim Brendel had been nominated for achieving 95 kills (although by

Oberleutnant Joachim Brendel, *Staffelkapitän* of 1./JG 51, takes time out to enjoy the cartoons on the back page of the latest issue of the *Berliner Illustrirte Zeitung* to arrive at the front

the time it was announced he too had already reached his century), while Oberleutnant Adolf Borchers of 11. *Staffel* got his for a total of 78.

One of December's three decorations was also posthumous. It went to Leutnant Josef Jennewein. Oberfeldwebel Kurt Tanzer received his award on the same 5 December. It was for a score of 'only' 35, but as a member of the *Stabsstaffel*, Tanzer had flown numerous ground-attack missions. The last Knight's Cross of the year was conferred upon Oberleutnant

Right
The long-serving *Kapitän* of 9. *Staffel*, Oberleutnant Maximilian Mayerl, was awarded the Knight's Cross just six days after leaving JG 51 on 8 December 1943. He is portrayed here (still wearing the *Jagdgeschwader 'Mölders'* cuff band) as a hauptmann and *Gruppenkommandeur* of I./EJG 1, the training unit he commanded for the remainder of the war

Far right
Oberfeldwebel Otto Würfel's 'Black 4' was inadvertently rammed by fellow Oberfeldwebel Heinrich Dittlmann during a hectic dogfight near Rogatchev on 23 February 1944. Both pilots were reported missing, and the 79-victory Würfel was subsequently awarded the Knight's Cross. Although he had in fact survived the mid-air collision, Würfel died in Soviet captivity on 22 December 1944

Although the runway is by now almost devoid of snow, these two Bf 109G-6s of the *Gruppenstab* I./JG 51 still wear full winter camouflage as they line up for another *Jabo* mission. 'Black double chevron' in the background is the mount of *Gruppenkommandeur* Major Erich Leie

Maximilian Mayerl for the 66 victories he had achieved while serving with the *Geschwader*, latterly as Kapitän of 9. *Staffel* (another *Jabo* specialist, Mayerl had in fact relinquished command of 9./JG 51 to Leutnant Günther Schack and taken up a training post just six days before his award was announced on 14 December).

Early 1944 found I. and III./JG 51 deployed to either side of the Rollbahn, at Bobruisk and Polozk respectively, while IV. *Gruppe* still remained on the southern sector under *Luftflotte* 4. Bobruisk was also the base of the Spanish *4a Escuadrilla Azul*, and it was here that the latter was joined by the first contingent of the replacement *5a Escuadrilla* towards the end of January. Since its arrival in Russia on the day *Zitadelle* was launched, *4a Escuadrilla* had claimed 73 enemy aircraft destroyed at a cost of seven pilots killed and three wounded. Its tour officially ended on 23 February. By this time, however, the Spanish government had already requested, and received, permission from Hitler, to withdraw all its forces from the eastern front. The *5a Escuadrilla Azul* was therefore recalled to Spain in March. It had flown just 86 sorties, which had produced no kills but had seen one pilot downed in combat.

With the situation on the central sector temporarily stabilised ('bogged down' would perhaps be a more accurate description), the opportunity was taken to complete JG 51's conversion back onto the Bf 109. I. *Gruppe* returned to Deblin-Irena, in Poland to exchange its Fw 190s for *Gustavs* during February, with III./JG 51 following suit in March. Only the *Stabsstaffel* retained its Focke-Wulfs.

The heavy burden being borne by IV./JG 51 on the southern sector was reflected in its casualty figures. Between August 1943 and the end of April 1944, the *Geschwader* lost 72 pilots killed, missing or captured – 31 of them came from the ranks of IV. *Gruppe* alone. Nor were these casualties all inexperienced tyros. The *Geschwader* was still suffering a worrying rate of attrition among its higher scorers. Of the eight Knight's Crosses won by JG 51 in the first four months of 1944, exactly half were awarded posthumously, with two going to pilots whose totals, coincidentally, had both reached 81 (for full details see Appendix 2).

April also brought the first Oak Leaves since the summer of 1942. After being wounded in Tunisia and spending six months in hospital, 'Toni' Hafner had finally returned to ops at the end of August 1943. He did not

Wearing the Knight's Cross newly awarded on 8 April 1944, Leutnant Anton 'Toni' Lindner had first joined JG 51 back in December 1939. He would end the war with 73 confirmed victories, and discharging twin duties as *Kapitän* of both the *Stabsstaffel* and 15./JG 51

Pictured here as an unteroffizier shortly after joining IV. *Gruppe* in 1942, Leutnant Rudolf Wagner was honoured with one of the four posthumous Knight's Crosses of early 1944 after being reported missing in action near Zhitomir, on the southern sector, on 11 December 1943

rejoin his old unit (II./JG 51, then undergoing anti-bomber training in the *Reich*), but was posted instead to III. *Gruppe* on the central sector of the eastern front. Oberfeldwebel Hafner had lost none of his old skills, however, and on 15 October he had achieved his century. On 1 March 1944 he was commissioned, and on 10 April the now Leutnant Anton Hafner scored victory 134, which earned him the Oak Leaves the following day.

Also a member of III./JG 51 and close on Hafner's heels, Leutnant Günther Schack, only recently awarded the Knight's Cross for 116 kills, had since added 17 more. His total of 133 won him the Oak Leaves on 20 April. With *Experten* such as these, it is perhaps not surprising that JG 51 was able to announce its 8000th victory of the war on 4 May.

The spring of 1944 witnessed several changes in command. On 30 March Oberstleutnant Karl-Gottfried Nordmann, the *Geschwader's* longest serving *Kommodore*, had departed to take up the post of *Jafü Ostpreussen* (Fighter-leader East Prussia). He was replaced on 1 April by Major Fritz Losigkeit, hitherto the *Kommandeur* of III. *Gruppe*. The officer selected to head III./JG 51 in Losigkeit's stead was Hauptmann Diethelm von Eichel-Streiber, who had been the *Kapitän* of the *Stabsstaffel* (and 6./JG 51 before that) since the autumn of 1942.

The announcement of the Oak Leaves for Leutnant Anton Hafner on 11 April 1944 resulted in a mock ceremony at Terespol, with Leutnant Kurt Tanzer pinning a wooden facsimile award on the irrepressible 'Toni' Hafner, who was then carried shoulder-high around the airfield

The actual ceremony at the *Führer's* HQ a few days later was a much more sober and sedate affair, with nine of the Luftwaffe's top *Experten* lining up to receive the Oak Leaves from the hands of Adolf Hitler, followed by congratulations from their C-in-C Hermann Göring. From the right, these leading *experten* are Leutnants Anton Hafner (JG 51), Otto Kittel (JG 54), Günther Schack (JG 51) and Oberleutnant Emil Lang (JG 54)

And on 8 May Major Hans-Ekkehard Bob was posted away to take command of II./JG 3 in Defence of the Reich. His replacement as *Kommandeur* of IV./JG 51 was Hauptmann Heinz Lange, another veteran *Staffelkapitän* who had been leading 3./JG 51 also since as far back as October 1942.

By the second half of May IV./JG 51 had withdrawn to Lemberg (Lvov), in the western Ukraine. On the central sector, I. *Gruppe* had returned to Orsha, alongside the Rollbahn, while the *Stabsstaffel* and III./JG 51 were further to the rear on a field near Brest-Litovsk, close to the Polish border. The uneasy peace that had descended on the central sector was ominous. The Red Army was clearly gathering its forces for another major offensive. Everybody knew it was the calm before the storm, but no-one could possibly have envisaged with what overwhelming strength and ferocity that storm would break.

Hitler had certainly abandoned all thoughts of a fourth summer offensive of his own in the east. His problems were now much nearer home. So much so, in fact, that at the end of May 1944 every *Jagdgruppe* fighting on the eastern front was ordered to give up one of its *Staffeln* for redeployment back to the homeland and incorporation into the Defence of the Reich organisation.

Major Fritz Losigkeit was appointed *Geschwaderkommodore* of JG 51 after the departure of Karl-Gottfried Nordmann

The three *Staffeln* of JG 51 selected for transfer were 2., 7. and 12. These became 16./JG 3, 8./JG 1 and 4./JG 302 respectively, and, as such, play no further part in the *Geschwader's* history. For the first few weeks with their new *Gruppen*, however, at least two of the *Staffeln*, having quickly converted back onto Fw 190s, continued to operate under their original designations.

It was thus still as 7./JG 51 that the ex-Mölders pilots accompanied II./JG 1 post-haste to Normandy on 7 June. They claimed 13 Allied fighters over the invasion beachhead in the month that followed, but it cost them 12 of their own killed. Although thrown in at the deep end of Reich's Defence as part of IV.(*Sturm*)/JG 3, Oberleutnant Horst Haase's 2./JG 51 was far more successful. Before finally being redesignated on 10 August, its pilots had been credited with the destruction of no fewer than 44 US heavy bombers against ten killed and four wounded (see *Osprey Aviation Elite Units 20 - Luftwaffe Sturmgruppen* for further details).

Only Oberleutnant Ferdinand Kray's 12./JG 51 retained its Bf 109s and underwent redesignation immediately upon joining I./JG 302 (the original 4./JG 302 having already become part of JG 300). Its initial role would be to fly top cover for the other *Staffeln* of its new parent *Gruppe* in defence of Austrian airspace.

Oberleutnant Walter Wever, erstwhile *Kapitän* of 3. *Staffel*, wearing the Knight's Cross awarded after his posting to JG 7. Wever was the son of Generalleutnant Walter Wever, the Luftwaffe's first Chief of Air Staff, who was an ardent believer in the strategic bomber concept. When he was killed in an air crash on 3 June 1936, official support for a long-range heavy bomber for the Luftwaffe effectively died with him

But this was not all. Early in June another order went the rounds of all the eastern front *Jagdstaffeln* demanding that each give up two of its more experienced pilots (*Schwarmführer* preferred!) for distribution throughout the Defence of the Reich units. It was thus a substantially depleted JG 51 that was suddenly faced with the appearance of an entirely new and unexpected enemy in Russian airspace. On 2 June a force of Fifteenth Air Force B-17s, with strong fighter escort, bombed marshalling yards in Hungary. Instead of returning to Italy, however, the Americans flew on to land at bases around Poltava, in the Ukraine. This was the first of the USAAF's Operation *Frantic* shuttle missions to Russia.

Rightly fearing more of the same – 'the threat of *Viermots* appearing overhead did wonders for our dispersal and camouflage', one pilot wryly noted – JG 51 began practising anti-bomber missions, this time with He 177s playing the part of the enemy. Its foresight paid off, for on 21 June UK-based B-17s of the Eighth Air Force bombed oil targets south of Berlin, before continuing on eastwards towards the Poltava complex.

I. and III./JG 51 happened to be flying another practice mission at the time, and their fuel tanks were almost empty when ground control reported the approach of the US formation. Ordering the *Stabsstaffel* to take off and join them, Major Losigkeit led his fighters into a frontal attack on the B-17s. Only one bomber was downed – by Leutnant Walter Wever, the *Kapitän* of 3. *Staffel* – before, in the *Kommodore's* own words, 'it started raining Mustangs!'

I./JG 51 was scattered, but Major Losigkeit managed to hold III. *Gruppe* together and engage the P-51s. Two of the American fighters were shot down, one crash-landing right on the edge of III./JG 51's base at Bobruisk. In it was found a map detailing the course to be followed into Russia, and revealing the exact locations of the Poltava airfields. *Gruppenkommandeur* von Eichel-Streiber immediately had the map sent to *Luftflotte* 6 HQ at Priluki. Once the information had been corroborated by a reconnaissance He 177 tailing the US formation, a Luftwaffe bombing raid was organised. During the night of 21/22 June a combined force of He 111s and Ju 88s attacked Poltava, destroying 44 B-17s on the ground and damaging a further 26.

The Luftwaffe was given no opportunity to celebrate this rare success. At 0500 hrs the following morning Soviet artillery began to thunder all along the central sector. Timed to coincide with the third anniversary of *Barbarossa*, and code-named Operation *Bagration* in honour of Russian Marshal Bagration, who had been mortally wounded before Moscow in 1812, the Red Army's great summer offensive had begun. In 12 days Army Group Centre lost 25 divisions. The front was torn apart as the Germans were driven out of Russia and back into Poland. Nearly a third of a million troops were lost. The eastern front was no longer a front, more a loosely linked chain of scattered armies each fighting its own bitter delaying action. It was the beginning of the end for every one of them – and for JG 51.

Major Losigkeit's units were in the very eye of the storm. Their three bases, Orsha (*Stabsstaffel* and I. *Gruppe*), Bobruisk (III.) and Mogilev (IV.) lay in an arc to the immediate south of the Rollbahn. This placed them between the inner jaws of the giant pincer movement that was rapidly developing as the Red Army closed in on its first major objective, Minsk, the capital of White Russia, and western terminus of the supply highway. The *Geschwader's* pilots fought hard. On 23 June they claimed 43 enemy machines without loss, 23 of them being credited to the Focke-Wulfs of the *Stabsstaffel* alone. But such figures were but a drop in the ocean against an opponent that was estimated to be hurling some 4500 aircraft daily against the shattered central sector.

On 28 June Leutnant Anton Hafner, now *Kapitän* of 8. *Staffel*, achieved his 150th kill. With his own machine damaged, he had to make an emergency landing behind enemy lines. Despite his injuries, he managed to get back on foot to friendly territory.

Minsk was recaptured by the Russians on 3 July. Forced onto the retreat, the *Geschwader's* casualties began to mount. Two *Staffelkapitäne* fell victim to ground fire. Leutnant Walter Wever of 3./JG 51 was brought down wounded on 10 July. Four days later the Focke-Wulf of the *Stabsstaffel's* Hauptmann Edwin Thiel took a direct flak hit in the right wing when at a height of only 200 metres. The machine immediately flipped over its left wing and plunged straight into a wood.

The months of May and June had each seen the award of a single Knight's Cross – one posthumous, the other to a pilot already reported missing. July's sole decoration went to Fahnenjunker-Oberfeldwebel (NCO officer candidate) Bernhard Vechtel of IV. *Gruppe* for 93 victories. By the end of the month the *Geschwader's* losses since the launch of *Bagration* totalled 15 killed or missing and ten wounded. But due to the many enforced moves and consequent servicing difficulties, materiel attrition over the same period had been even higher. From a combined establishment of 122 machines as of 26 June, the three *Gruppen* could now muster just 19 serviceable fighters between them!

The intense pressure eased somewhat during August as the Red Army began to outstrip its lines of supply. It was at this time that the order calling for every *Jagdgruppe* to be increased in strength from three *Staffeln* to four came into effect. Unlike II./JG 51, currently down in southeastern

Members of the *Stabsstaffel* photographed with their *Kapitän*, Leutnant Gustav Sturm (fifth from right), at Jürgensfeld in August 1944. Of the ten pilots shown here, exactly half would survive the last eight months of the war. Among the gathering are two future Knight's Cross winners, namely Oberfeldwebel Helmut Schönfelder (second from left) and Leutnant Wilhelm Hübner (third from right). But 'Willi' Hübner was also one of the five casualties, his Fw 190A-8 'Black 22' being shot down over Neukuhren in East Prussia on 8 April 1945

Europe, however, the *Geschwader's* three eastern front *Gruppen* failed to comply with instructions (whether they were temporarily exempt or simply unable to do so is not clear). In fact, as a result of May's cull of *Staffeln* for Reich's Defence duties, each of Losigkeit's *Gruppen* was still composed of only two *Staffeln*! But, perhaps with a view to reinforcement sometime in the future, these did undergo some renumbering. I./JG 51 retained its 1. and 3. *Staffeln* as before, but III. *Gruppe* now consisted of 9. and 10. (ex-8.) *Staffeln*, and IV. *Gruppe's* 10. and 11. *Staffeln* were redesignated to become 13. and 14./JG 51.

By mid-August the *Geschwader's* strength had been split. While Major Losigkeit's *Stab* and III./JG 51 were transferred up to Tilsit, in East Prussia, close to the Lithuanian border, I. and IV. *Gruppen* were based near Modlin, to the north of the Polish capital, Warsaw. It was from Modlin that IV./JG 51 flew Stuka-escort missions against the Polish underground army's uprising in Warsaw during the latter half of August and into September. And on 18 September both I. and IV. *Gruppen* were sent up against US heavy bombers reported approaching from the northwest. The Eighth Air Force was engaged on another of its shuttle missions to the Soviet Union, but this time the B-17s were carrying not bombs but arms and supplies for the Poles fighting in Warsaw.

The two *Gruppen* attempted to form up for a frontal attack on the Flying Fortresses, but their 28 Bf 109s were scattered by the bombers' 140-strong Mustang escort. Only one B-17 was brought down, this being victory 123 for Oberleutnant Günther Josten, the *Kapitän* of 3. *Staffel* (Josten's 100th kill had been an Il-2 claimed on 20 July).

Meanwhile, up in East Prussia, III./JG 51 – commanded since 1 September by Hauptmann Joachim Brendel – was fully stretched covering the German ground withdrawal through the Baltic states and

A pipe-smoking Oberfeldwebel Günther Josten photographed in the early spring of 1944. The 390th BG B-17 he was to claim on 18 September was the only heavy bomber among his final total of 178 confirmed victories (more than 60 of which were heavily-armoured Il-2 *Sturmoviks*)

guarding coastal convoys from Soviet air attack. On 22 September its pilots downed a complete formation of six Red Air Force Boston torpedo-bombers off the Courland coast before the enemy's fighter escort could intervene. But it was over East Prussia that the *Geschwader* was to suffer its greatest loss. While dogfighting at low level with a group of Soviet Yak-9s east of Insterburg on 17 October, Oberleutnant Anton Hafner's 'Black 1' clipped a tree and crashed. With 204 victories to his credit – he had topped the double century two days earlier – 'Toni' Hafner, *Kapitän* of 10. *Staffel*, was – and would remain – JG 51's highest ever scorer.

October found the *Geschwader* operating over all three major areas of the eastern front. To the north I./JG 51 had joined the *Stabsstaffel* and III. *Gruppe* in the Baltic coastal regions. In the centre IV./JG 51 remained at Modlin, close to the Polish capital, where, during the course of the month, it would claim 102 victories at a cost of just four killed and two wounded. And on the southern flank, based at Felsöabrany, in Hungary, II./JG 51 was now officially part of *Luftflotte* 4, but continuing to wage its

Future Knight's Cross winner Oberfeldwebel Heinz Marquardt (left) of 13. *Staffel* ended his war flying the Fw 190D-9. On 24 April 1945 he downed four Soviet Yak-3s during a routine D-9 delivery flight! The last of his 121 victories was a Spitfire IX claimed over Schwerin on 1 May 1945, after which action he himself had to bale out wounded

two-front war against the Russians in the east and the US Fifteenth Air Force flying up from Italy. It was II. *Gruppe's Kommandeur*, Major Karl Rammelt, who received October's only Knight's Cross.

The onset of a particularly bad spell of weather along much of the eastern front in November offered the *Geschwader* a welcome respite from ops, and also gave the units the opportunity to accelerate their conversion from Bf 109G-6s to G-14s. The actuation of 15. *Staffel* in Poland on 1 November brought IV./JG 51 back up to three-*Staffel* establishment.

Oberfeldwebel Fritz Lüddecke, seen here describing a recent dogfight to Kurt Tanzer, was another of the *Stabsstaffel's* veteran *Jabo Experten* to fall victim to Soviet anti-aircraft fire

This *Gruppe* also won three of the year's last four Knight's Crosses. *Kommandeur* Hauptmann Heinz Lange and Oberfeldwebel Heinz Marquardt both received theirs on 18 November (for 70 and 89 victories respectively). Leutnant Peter Kalden, *Kapitän* of 13. *Staffel*, was honoured on 6 December for 64. The fourth went posthumously to the *Stabsstaffel's* Oberfeldwebel Fritz Lüddecke, whose Fw 190A-8, hit by anti-aircraft fire over East Prussia on 10 August, had exploded into a fireball just above the ground as he was attempting a belly-landing.

November's only casualties were two leutnants of 6. *Staffel*, brought down during a dogfight with P-51s over Lake Balaton, in Hungary, on 6 November. Exactly one month later II./JG 51 lost four more pilots in action against a formation of B-24s, escorted by P-38 Lightnings, attacking marshalling yards near Hungary's border with Austria. And on 23 December the *Gruppenkommandeur* himself, Major Karl Rammelt, was severely wounded in action northwest of Budapest.

Rammelt was replaced at the head of II. *Gruppe* by Oberleutnant Otto Schultz, hitherto the *Kapitän* of 6. *Staffel*. This was not the only change of command in the closing days of 1944. On 28 December I./JG 51's Major Erich Leie was appointed *Kommodore* of JG 77. The *Geschwader's* sole surviving Oak Leaves wearer, Hauptmann Günther Schack, was brought in from 9. *Staffel* to take over I. *Gruppe* in his stead.

On 13 January the Red Army had launched a winter offensive that, in the space of little more than ten weeks, was to take it all the way to the banks of the River Oder, only 80 kilometres from the centre of Berlin. Against such a cataclysmic backdrop, the formation of two new *Staffeln* – 2. and 11./JG 51 – on 15 January was almost an irrelevance. But they did at least serve to bring both I. and III. *Gruppen* back up to three-*Staffel* strength.

By the second half of January the whole *Geschwader*, with the exception of II. *Gruppe*, was deployed along the Baltic coast, *Stab*, I. and IV. *Gruppen* (the latter having escaped from Modlin under Soviet artillery bombardment) based at Danzig, and III./JG 51, whose *Kommandeur*, Hauptmann Joachim Brendel, had just been awarded the Oak Leaves for his 156 victories, further to the east around Königsberg. Here they would remain almost until the end.

At first their missions included flying escort for ground-attack aircraft and trying to protect the hundreds of thousands of civilian refugees fleeing westwards by land and sea. But their soaring losses (some 40 pilots killed or missing between mid-January and mid-March), coupled with the worsening fuel crisis, soon reduced them to carrying out little more than individual fighter reconnaissance sorties.

Despite the critical situation, the *Gruppen* were still being supplied with replacement aircraft. During February several brand new Bf 109G-10s and K-4s were delivered to III. and IV./JG 51 respectively. Decorations were still being conferred as well. On 18 February the *Stabsstaffel's* Leutnant Wilhelm Hübner was awarded the Knight's Cross, and exactly one month later the *Geschwader's* last Oak Leaves went to Oberleutnant Günther Josten, whose total was then standing at 161.

By this time the Red Army was flooding into Pomerania, and the German-held enclaves around Danzig and Königsberg were completely cut off. With Danzig-Langfuhr airfield on the point of being overrun, the

Oberfeldwebel Helmut Schönfelder flew 172 *Jabo* missions as a member of the *Stabsstaffel*. Here, he poses for the camera while his winter-camouflaged Fw 190A-8 is readied for its next sortie. Note what appears to be an AB 250 bomb container on the aircraft's ventral rack

remnants of I. and IV. *Gruppen* received orders to evacuate – I./JG 51 was to move *east* by road, towing their aircraft(!), to join III. *Gruppe* in the Königsberg pocket. IV./JG 51 was to retire westwards by ship to Garz, on the island of Usedom, where it would be re-equipped with Fw 190A-8s and A-9s, plus a few 'long-nose' D-9s.

Meanwhile, in the south, II. *Gruppe* had been slowly retreating across Hungary. After supporting the ill-conceived counter-attack around Lake Balaton, ordered by the *Führer* in a forlorn attempt to halt the Red Army's advance on Vienna, II./JG 51 was itself back on Austrian soil by the end of March. Its last operation of the war, flown from Fels am Wagram on 9 April, was to escort Hs 129s on a mission to destroy oil tanks near Vienna to prevent their falling into Russian hands. Two pilots failed to return. Three days later the *Gruppe* was disbanded.

On that same 12 April Königsberg fell to the Soviets. I. and III. *Gruppen's* three(!) serviceable Bf 109s were on landing strips some distance outside the city. The end could not be far off. On 23 April I./JG 51 was disbanded, most of its pilots transferring to III. *Gruppe* which, incredibly, was reinforced by the addition of a new 12. *Staffel* the following day. But this was merely delaying the inevitable. Although yet more Bf 109G-10s were flown in, many were quickly destroyed on the ground by low-flying *Sturmoviks*. When the order to evacuate came on 5 May, only 15 aircraft could be made serviceable. With insufficient fuel to reach German territory, they were instructed to head for the Danish island of Bornholm, in the Baltic. Nine made it.

All of which left just the Focke-Wulfs of IV./JG 51. Early in April *Kommandeur* Major Heinz Lange had been appointed JG 51's sixth and final *Geschwaderkommodore* after Fritz Losigkeit had been ordered to take over at the head of JG 77 (the previous incumbent – Oberstleutnant Erich

Late model *Gustavs*, almost certainly of JG 51, abandoned in East Prussia at the end of the war

Leie, ex-I./JG 51 – having been killed in action against Yak-9s on 7 March). IV. *Gruppe* was now under the command of Oberleutnant Günther Josten. Operating from bases to the east of Berlin, its main task was to escort the Luftwaffe's few remaining bombers and ground-assault aircraft attacking the Red Army poised along the River Oder ready for the final assault on the German capital. It also flew cover for the Ju 88 *Mistel* combinations trying to knock out the Oder bridges. But when an appeal was made for volunteers to undertake suicide missions by deliberately crashing bomb-laden Ju 88s into the bridges, none of the *Gruppe's* pilots felt inclined to respond.

Major Heinz Lange served briefly as the sixth and final *Kommodore* of the *Geschwader*, before returning to his long-standing command of IV./JG 51 to oversee its surrender to the Western allies

Towards the end of April, with the *Geschwaderstab* being disbanded, Major Lange returned to take over the *Gruppe* again. By this time IV./JG 51 included one Oak Leaves and six Knight's Cross wearers within its ranks. With this wealth of talent – some of them flying what was arguably the world's finest piston-engined fighter, the Fw 190D-9 – it is little wonder that the *Gruppe* continued to score almost right up until the very end. In three weeks in front of Berlin its pilots claimed no fewer than 115 enemy aircraft destroyed for the loss of five of their own.

Heinz Marquardt (right) surveys the damage done to his Fw 190D-9 when he accidentally ran it into a drainage ditch at the start of a short transfer flight between fields to the north of Berlin on 30 April 1945. With no replacement available for that splintered wooden propeller, 'White 11' had to be blown up to prevent its falling into Russian hands

A be-medalled but clearly dejected Leutnant Kurt Tanzer, *Kapitän* of 13. Staffel, contemplates his final flight from Parchim/Redlin to Flensburg on 2 May to await the arrival of British forces. Note the bomb container on the D-9 – possibly Tanzer's own 'White 1' – in the background

But no amount of experience could influence events now. There was even one last-ditch proposal that the *Gruppe* should operate from the very heart of Berlin itself, using a stretch of the capital's main East-West Axis thoroughfare as a runway. But this came to nothing when Hitler expressly forbade chopping down the avenue of trees that lined the road either side! And on 2 May – the day Berlin finally capitulated – IV./JG 51 was ordered to fly to Flensburg, in Schleswig-Holstein, to await the arrival of British forces. Flensburg was a collecting point for large numbers of surrendered aircraft, and the members of the *Gruppe* were put to work by the RAF rendering them unfit to fly. 'We were' commented one pilot, 'a sort of disarmament *Kommando*'.

It was an ignominious end to what had once been the Luftwaffe's most successful *Jagdgeschwader*.

Late model Focke-Wulfs – including at least two Fw 190D-9s – of IV./JG 51 lined up at Flensburg at the end of the war

POSTSCRIPT – WERNER WHO?

Little more than a decade after the defeat of May 1945, when the Cold War between the eastern and western *bloc* powers in Europe was at its height, West Germany was re-armed and invited to take its place alongside the other nations in NATO (the North Atlantic Treaty Organisation).

To help foster a sense of tradition and continuity, four *Geschwader* of the new *Bundesluftwaffe* were subsequently given honour titles. Three of these were names of World War 1 fighter pilots – Richthofen, Immelmann and Boelcke. The fourth choice, and the only one relating directly to World War 2, was more contentious.

It was on 22 November 1973, the 32nd anniversary of the death of Werner Mölders, that *Jagdgeschwader* 74, then flying F-104 Starfighters and based at Neuburg-on-the-Danube, was formally awarded its honour title as the *Geschwader 'Mölders'*. In a ceremony attended by a large number of invited guests, including immediate members of the Mölders family and both 'Onkel Theo' Osterkamp and Dr Heinz Lange, the first and last *Kommodores* of the wartime JG 51, Generalleutnant Günther Rall, the then *Inspekteur der Bundesluftwaffe*, symbolically attached the first *'Mölders'* cuff-title to the sleeve of Oberst Rudolf Erlemann, JG 74's Commanding Officer.

This was not the first time that the post-war *Bundeswehr* had commemorated the name of Mölders. The previous year a Luftwaffe radar base at Visselhövede, on Lüneburg Heath, had been named the *'Mölders Kaserne'* ('Mölders Barracks'). And four years prior to that, on 13 April 1968, the Mölders family had been honoured guests in America for the launch of the US-built *Charles F Adams* class guided-missile destroyer D186 *Mölders*, ordered by the *Bundesmarine* (Federal German Navy).

General der Jagdflieger **Oberst Werner Mölders during a tour of inspection of the eastern front on 7 October 1941**

This resurrection of one of the Third Reich's most celebrated war heroes did not go down at all well with many of Germany's left-wing politicians of the period, however. And after years of protesting, they got their way. The blow finally fell on 28 January 2005 when Germany's Minister of Defence, Dr Peter Struck, announced that the name Mölders was to be removed from the *Bundeswehr* roll of honour titles.

The minister's decision was based upon a plenary session of the German parliament, which had sat seven years earlier on 24 April 1998. This meeting, which coincided almost to the day with the anniversary of the bombing of Guernica during the Spanish Civil War over 60 years earlier, had prompted its members 'in a gesture of conciliation' to acknowledge 'Germany's guilt and responsibility and thereby strengthen the foundations for a spirit of friendly and peaceful cooperation between the peoples'.

It was further recommended that no German who had served in the *Legion Condor* (and who had thus fought against the legitimate Republican Spanish government and its communist supporters) should be honoured in any way in today's Germany. And there the matter might have rested, had not a group of activists in the Neuburg region, backed by certain sections of the media, been determined to keep the issue alive.

Against whom, other than Werner Mölders, the original plenary meeting recommendation was aimed is difficult to imagine. His was certainly the most famous name affected by the proposal. And the media were not about to let anyone forget it. One television magazine described Mölders as 'a prototypical Nazi officer who volunteered with enthusiasm to join the war against the Spanish civil population'.

It mattered not that Mölders had been sent to Spain *after* the bombing of Guernica, or that the war he fought there was waged not against the Spanish civil population but against Republican air and ground forces. Nor could he, by any stretch of the imagination, be described as a 'typical Nazi'. He was not only avowedly non-political, but deeply religious and a devout Catholic. The awards and accolades bestowed upon him by the leaders of the Third Reich resulted from his prowess as a fighter pilot, and not from any adherence on his part to their unholy cause.

The long-running, politically motivated witch-hunt outraged most of Germany's surviving World War 2 veterans, as well as many who had served in the post-war *Bundeswehr*. But with that nation's innate respect for those placed in authority above them, their reactions did not go much beyond icily written letters of protest. Needless to say, these fell on deaf ears. The deed had been done. In a move that would not have been out of place in Stalinist Russia of the 1930s, Werner Mölders had been officially declared a non-person in the eyes of the German ruling establishment.

The Socialist politicians had had their cake. But now they wanted to eat it too. In a letter from the defence minister's office addressed to Mölders' 91-year old widow the good lady was assured, with breathtaking condescension, that it was 'nothing personal'.

The *Geschwader 'Mölders'* honour title cuff-band worn by members of the post-war *Jagdgeschwader* 74 from 22 November 1973 to 28 January 2005

APPENDICES

APPENDIX 1

COMMANDING OFFICERS

Kommodoren

Osterkamp, *Oberst* Theo	19/9/39	to 23/7/40
Mölders, *Obstlt* Werner	27/7/40	to 19/7/41
Beckh, *Obstlt* Friedrich	19/7/41	to 10/4/42
Lützow, *Maj* Günther (acting)	9/41	to 8/11/41
Nordmann, *Obstlt* Karl-Gottfried	10/4/42	to 30/3/44
Müncheberg, *Hptm* Joachim (acting)	8/42	to 9/42
Losigkeit, *Maj* Fritz	1/4/44	to 31/3/45
Lange, *Maj* Heinz	12/4/45	to 28/4/45

Gruppenkommandeure

I./JG 51

Ibel, *Maj* Max	15/3/37	to 31/10/38
von Berg, *Maj* Ernst *Freiherr*	1/11/38	to 22/9/39
Brustellin, *Hptm* Hans-Heinrich	23/9/39	to 17/10/40
Joppien, *Hptm* Hermann-Friedrich	18/10/40	to 25/8/41 (†)
Hachfeld, *Hptm* Wilhelm	25/8/41	to 2/5/42
Fözö, *Hptm* Josef	3/5/42	to 31/5/42 (W)
Krafft, *Hptm* Heinrich	1/6/42	to 14/12/42 (†)
Busch, *Hptm* Rudolf	15/12/42	to 17/1/43 (†)
Leie, *Maj* Erich	18/1/43	to 28/12/44
Schack, *Hptm* Günther	29/12/44	to 23/4/45

II./JG 51

Burgaller, *Maj* Ernst Günther	1/11/39	to 2/2/40 (†)
Matthes, *Hptm* Günther	3/2/40	to 20/2/41
Fözö, *Hptm* Josef	21/2/41	to 11/7/41 (W)
von Bonin, *Hptm* Hubertus (acting)	11/7/41	to 8/8/41 (W)
Hohagen, *Oblt* Erich (acting)	9/8/41	to 4/9/41 (W)
Grasser, *Hptm* Hartmann	4/9/41	to 6/6/43
Rammelt, *Maj* Karl	6/6/43	to 23/12/44 (W)
Schultz, *Oblt* Otto	24/12/44	to 12/4/45

III./JG 51

Lehmann, *Maj* Siegfried	15/7/39	to 18/9/39
Trautloft, *Hptm* Hannes	23/9/39	to 24/8/40
Oesau, *Hptm* Walter	24/8/40	to 10/11/40
Leppla, *Hptm* Richard	11/11/40	to 7/8/42 (W)
Wehnelt, *Oblt* Herbert (acting)	7/8/42	to 11/42
Schnell, *Hptm* Karl-Heinz	11/42	to 22/6/43
Losigkeit, *Hptm* Fritz	26/6/43	to 30/3/44
von Eichel-Streiber, *Hptm* Diethelm	1/4/44	to 24/8/44
Brendel, *Hptm* Joachim	1/9/44	to 8/5/45

IV./JG 51

Osterkamp, *Obstlt* Theo	1/7/38	to 7/38
Janke, *Hptm* Johannes	7/38	to 18/2/41
Keitel, *Oblt* Hans-Karl	20/2/41	to 26/2/41 (†)
Beckh, *Maj* Friedrich	1/3/41	to 19/7/41
Nordmann, *Hptm* Karl-Gottfried	20/7/41	to 9/4/42
Knauth, *Hptm* Hans	10/4/42	to 28/2/43
Resch, *Maj* Rudolf	1/3/43	to 11/7/43 (†)
Moritz, *Hptm* Wilhelm (acting)	12/7/43	to 31/7/43
Bob, *Maj* Hans-Ekkehard	1/8/43	to 8/5/44
Lange, *Maj* Heinz	9/5/44	to 11/4/45
Josten, *Oblt* Günther	12/4/45	to 28/4/45
Lange, *Maj* Heinz	29/4/45	to 8/5/45

(†) – Killed, Missing or Failed to Return
(W) – Wounded

APPENDIX 2

AWARD WINNERS

Date	Name	Unit	Award	Score at of Time of Award	Final Score	Fate
20/8/40	Oesau, *Hptm* Walter	7.	KC	20	118	KiA
20/8/40	Tietzen, *Hptm* Horst*	5.	KC	20	20	KiA
16/9/40	Joppien, *Oblt* Hermann Friedrich	1.	KC	21	70	KiA
21/9/40	Mölders, *Maj* Werner	51	OL	40	101	KAS
19/10/40	Priller, *Oblt* Josef	6.	KC	20	101	
23/4/41	Joppien, *Hptm* Hermann Friedrich	I.	OL	40	70	KiA
22/6/41	Mölders, *Obstlt* Werner	51	S	72	101	KAS
2/7/41	Bär, *Lt* Heinz	1.	KC	27	221	
2/7/41	Fözö, *Hptm* Josef	II.	KC	22	24	W
16/7/41	Mölders, *Obstlt* Werner	51	D	101	101	KAS
16/7/41	Staiger, *Oblt* Hermann	7.	KC	25	63	
27/7/41	Kolbow, *Oblt* Hans*	5.	KC	27	27	KiA
27/7/41	Leppla, *Hptm* Richard	III.	KC	27	68	
1/8/41	Nordmann, *Oblt* Karl-Gottfried	IV.	KC	31	78	
1/8/41	Schnell, *Oblt* Karl-Heinz	9.	KC	29	72	
12/8/41	Fleig, *Lt* Erwin	1.	KC	26	66	PoW
12/8/41	Hoffmann, *Obfw* Heinrich	12.	KC	40	63	KiA
14/8/41	Bär, *Oblt* Heinz	12.	OL	60	221	
30/8/41	Huppertz, *Lt* Herbert	12.	KC	34	68	KiA
4/9/41	Grasser, *Oblt* Hartmann	5.	KC	29	103	
16/9/41	Nordmann, *Oblt* Karl-Gottfried	IV.	OL	59	78	
18/9/41	Beckh, *Maj* Friedrich	51	KC	27	41	MiA
5/10/41	Hohagen, *Oblt* Erich	II.	KC	30	55	
6/10/41	Beerenbrock, *Uffz* Franz-Josef	IV.	KC	42	117	PoW
6/10/41	Seelmann, *Lt* Georg	11.	KC	37	39	
19/10/41	Hoffmann, *Obfw* Heinrich*	12.	OL	63	63	KiA
17/11/41	Wagner, *Obfw* Edmund*	9.	KC	55	55	KiA
24/1/42	Gallowitsch, *Lt* Bernd	12.	KC	42	64	
16/2/42	Bär, *Hptm* Heinz	12.	S	90	221	
18/3/42	Krafft, *Oblt* Heinrich	3.	KC	46	78	KiA
18/3/42	Strelow, *Lt* Hans	5.	KC	52	68	KiA
19/3/42	Mink, *Obfw* Wilhelm	5.	KC	40	72	KiA
19/3/42	Tange, *Obfw* Otto	4.	KC	41	68	KiA
24/3/42	Strelow, *Lt* Hans	5.	OL	66	68	KiA
5/4/42	Höfemeier, *Obfw* Heinrich	1.	KC	41	96	KiA
3/8/42	Beerenbrock, *Obfw* Franz-Josef	10.	OL	102	117	PoW
21/8/42	Weismann, *Oblt* Ernst*	12.	KC	69	69	MiA
23/8/42	Hafner, *Fw* Anton	6.	KC	60	204	KiA
4/9/42	Klöpper, *Obfw* Heinrich	11.	KC	65	94	MiA
9/9/42	Müncheberg, *Hptm* Joachim	51	S	103	135	KiA
3/11/42	Knappe, *Uffz* Kurt	5.	KC	51	54	KiA
24/1/43	Friebel, *Obfw* Herbert	12.	KC	51	58	KiA
14/3/43	Rübell, *Oblt* Günther	5.	KC	43	47	
14/3/43	Schultz, *Obfw* Otto	4.	KC	51	73	
24/3/43	Böwing-Treuding, *Oblt* Wolfgang*	10.	KC	46	46	KiA

Date	Name	Unit	Award	Score at of Time of Award	Final Score	Fate
16/4/43	Thiel, *Oblt* Edwin	2.	KC	51	76	KiA
29/10/43	Schack, *Lt* Günther	8.	KC	116	174	
12/11/43	Strassl, *Obfw* Hubert*	8.	KC	67	67	KiA
12/11/43	Weber, *Oblt* Karl-Heinz	7.	KC	100	136	MiA
22/11/43	Borchers, *Hptm* Adolf	11.	KC	78	132	
22/11/43	Brendel, *Oblt* Joachim	1.	KC	95	189	
5/12/43	Jennewein, *Lt* Josef*	2.	KC	86	86	MiA
5/12/43	Tanzer, *Obfw* Kurt	St.	KC	41	68	KiA
5/2/44	Josten, *Obfw* Günther	3.	KC	84	178	
29/2/44	Leber, *Obfw* Heinz*	2.	KC	54	54	KiA
29/2/44	Romm, *Obfw* Oskar	1.	KC	76	92	
26/3/44	Wagner, *Lt* Rudolf*	12.	KC	81	81	MiA
5/4/44	von Eichel-Streiber, *Hptm* Diethelm	St.	KC	71	96	
5/4/44	Puschmann, *Hptm* Herbert*	6.	KC	54	54	KiA
6/4/44	Lücke, *Oblt* Hermann*	9.	KC	81	81	KiA
8/4/44	Lindner, *Lt* Anton	St.	KC	62	73	
11/4/44	Hafner, *Lt* Anton	St.	OL	134	204	KiA
20/4/44	Schack, *Lt* Günther	9.	OL	133	174	
4/5/44	Würfel, *Obfw* Otto	9.	KC	79	79	PoW
9/6/44	Gaiser, *Lt* Otto*	10.	KC	74	74	MiA
27/7/44	Vechtel, *Fj Obfw* Bernhard	11.	KC	93	108	
24/10/44	Rammelt, *Hptm* Karl	II.	KC	40	46	
18/11/44	Lange, *Hptm* Heinz	IV.	KC	70	70	
18/11/44	Lüddecke, *Obfw* Fritz*	St.	KC	50	50	KiA
18/11/44	Marquardt, *Obfw* Heinz	13.	KC	89	121	
6/12/44	Kalden, *Lt* Peter	13.	KC	64	84	PoW
14/1/45	Brendel, *Hptm* Joachim	III.	OL	156	189	
28/2/45	Hübner, *Lt* Wilhelm	St.	KC	?	62	KiA
28/3/45	Josten, *Oblt* Günther	3.	OL	161	178	
31/3/45	Schönfelder, *Obfw* Helmut	St.	KC	?	56	
7/4/45	Dombacher, *Lt* Kurt	12.	KC	?	68	
9/4/45	Rauch, *Fj Obfw* Alfred	St.	KC	53	60	

Key

KiA – Killed in Action
MiA – Missing in Action
KAS – Killed on Active Service
PoW – Prisoner of War
* – awarded posthumously
St. – *Stabsstaffel*
KC – Knight's Cross
OL – Oak leaves
S – Swords
D – Diamonds

COLOUR PLATES

1

He 51B 'White 1' of Hauptmann Georg Meyer, *Staffelkapitän* 2./JG 135, Bad Aibling, February 1938

Resplendent in the pale blue trim used to identify aircraft of JG 135, and wearing the white bands around its cowling and aft fuselage indicating 2. *Staffel*, Meyer's machine displays – perhaps not altogether by chance – the colours of its home state Bavaria. After claiming a single kill during the 'Phoney War', Meyer took up a training post with JFS (Fighter School) Fürth in August 1940.

2

Bf 109B 'Yellow 7' of 3./JG 135, Wien (Vienna)-Aspern, March 1938

The first *Staffel* to equip with Messerschmitt Bf 109s, 3./JG 135's *Bertas*, in their sombre dark green/black green camouflage finish, looked much more business-like than their colourful biplane predecessors. Only the retention of the *Gruppe* badge – the skull of a 'Kitzbühl chamois' – offered any clue as to the aircraft's parent unit.

3

Bf 109E-1 'Black Double Chevron' of Hauptmann Johannes Janke, *Gruppenkommandeur* I./JG 77, Kracow/Poland, September 1939

Depicted a fortnight into the Polish campaign, Janke's early *Emil* – Werk-Nr. 3250 – displays on its cowling the 'worn-out boot' emblem that he himself had introduced in mid-1939 to signify the many moves his *'Wanderzirkus'* was being called upon to make. Note also the *Gruppe's* small disc marking behind the fuselage cross, and the narrow aft fuselage band used by the unit to identify the aircraft of a formation leader.

4

Bf 109E-3 'White 1' of Oberleutnant Walter Oesau, *Staffelkapitän* 1./JG 20, Brandenburg-Briest, October 1939

The mount of an *Experte* in the making, this machine wears camouflage finish and national insignia very similar to that shown immediately above. The white 'bow and arrow' (black on later *hellblau* aircraft) is the emblem of 1. *Staffel*. The wavy bar aft of the fuselage cross had been applied to all I./JG 20 aircraft in the early autumn of 1939 in readiness for the unit's planned redesignation as III./JG 2 – which in the event never took place. Some 39 of Oesau's final total of 116 victories were claimed during his early service with I./JG 20 (III./JG 51).

5

Bf 109E 'Black Chevron, Triangle and Bar' I./JG 20, Bönninghardt, March 1940

By early 1940 the *Emils* of I./JG 20 had undergone several changes. The most obvious was the application of a *hellblau* camouflage finish, but note also the introduction of a new *Gruppe* badge – the 'Axe of the Lower-Rhine', occasioned by the move from the Berlin area to Bönninghardt in February 1940. The aircraft also boasts the transitional style of national insignia, namely a small fuselage cross with wide white borders, coupled with a tail Swastika still centred on the rudder hinge line. Initially thought to be the aircraft of *Kommandeur* Hannes Trautloft, the unusual command insignia are now believed to indicate this to be one of the machines of the *Gruppe's* six-strong HQ flight.

6

Bf 109E 'White 13' of Feldwebel Heinz Bär, 1./JG 51, Pihen, September 1940

Another *hellblau* machine, but this time with definitive 1940 national insignia and yellow tactical markings of the Battle of Britain period. Note the modified I. *Gruppe* badge (compare with profiles 1 and 2) and the 'Mickey Mouse' emblem of 1. *Staffel* below the cockpit. The numeral '13' usually denoted a *Staffel's* reserve aircraft, but in this instance it was the lucky number of future *Experte* Heinz Bär, whose eight victories shown here rise to 91 by the time he left JG 51 in May 1942.

7

Bf 109E 'Black 4' of 5./JG 51, Mardyck, Autumn 1940

By the closing stages of the Battle of Britain most machines had their 1940 *hellblau* finish toned down by dark green dappling of one form or another. This 5. Staffel *Jabo* – wearing II. Gruppe's 'Weeping raven' badge aft of the fuselage cross instead of a regulation horizontal bar – provides a typical example. Note the two aerial victories recorded on the tailfin.

8

Bf 109F 'Black Chevron Triangle' of Major Friedrich Beckh, *Gruppenkommandeur* IV./JG 51, Le Touquet, March 1941

When I./JG 77 was redesignated IV./JG 51 and began converting to Bf 109Fs – both in the winter of 1940-41 – their machines initially carried no distinguishing marks whatsoever (other than the original 'worn-out boot' device retained by some). As the only IV. *Gruppe* currently within the ranks of the *Jagdwaffe*, a new *Gruppe* symbol had to be devised. It took the form of a small cross repeated aft of the fuselage cross, and was soon being displayed as depicted here.

9

Bf 109F 'Black Chevron, Triangle and Bars' of Major Werner Mölders, *Geschwaderkommodore* JG 51, Mardyck, May 1941

Another innovation, introduced in April 1941, was the *Geschwader* badge. The design was the head of a bird of prey against a pale-blue disc (references differ as to the exact species, some maintaining that the bird shown is an Icelandic falcon, others that it is a buzzard). It is seen here on one of Mölders' several *Friedrichs*, which also sports a textbook set of *Kommodore's* insignia and 63 victory bars on its yellow rudder. The last of these victories, downed southwest of Boulogne on 15 April, was claimed as a Spitfire, but was more likely to have been a Hurricane of No 615 Sqn.

10

Bf 109F-2 'White 5' of Oberfeldwebel Heinrich Höfemeier, 1./JG 51, Starawies/Poland, June 1941

This distinctively dappled 'White 5' is believed to be the machine in which future Knight's Cross winner Heinrich Höfemeier was wounded after bringing down four SB-2 bombers on the opening day of *Barbarossa.* It wears the new *Geschwader* badge on the cowling and I. *Gruppe's* emblem below the windscreen, plus early eastern front yellow theatre markings.

11

Bf 109F-2 'Black 11' of Feldwebel Anton Lindner, 2./JG 51, Stara Bychov, July 1941

Oversprayed in much softer dapple, and minus the *Gruppe* badge, Anton Lindner's 'Black 11' is shown here armed with four 50-kg bombs on its ventral ETC rack. A highly successful *Jabo* pilot, Lindner had also amassed 73 confirmed aerial victories – and been awarded the Knight's Cross - by war's end.

12

Bf 109F-2 'White 11' of Feldwebel Werner Bielefeldt, 7./JG 51, Bobruisk-South, July 1941

Carrying no unit badges whatsoever, this 'White 11' does, however, bear a careful record of its pilot's successes to date – Bielefeldt's tenth victom was a Petlyakov Pe-2 bomber, downed northeast of Mogilev on 11 July. Note also the white vertical III. *Gruppe* bar aft of the fuselage cross, first introduced when III./JG 51 (the ex-I./JG 20) began converting from Bf 109Es to Fs in February 1941.

13

Bf 109F-2 'Black Double Chevron' of Oberleutnant Karl-Gottfried Nordmann, *Gruppenkommandeur* IV./JG 51, Shatalovka, August 1941

Pictured in mid-August, Nordmann's machine displays no indication of the fact that he was only days away from his half-century. But it *does* sport the *Geschwader* badge on the cowling, a regulation set of *Kommandeur's* chevrons, IV. *Gruppe's* cross on the rear fuselage and – harking back to the unit's earlier days as the *'Wanderzirkus'* – a small worn-out boot on a shield below the cockpit sill.

14

Bf 109F 'White 9' of 4./JG 51, Sezhinskaya, September 1941

Another machine offering more than a passing nod to its origins, 'White 1' still proudly carries a 'weeping raven' device behind the aft fuselage yellow band. But when re-equipping with Bf 109Fs in June 1941, II./JG 51 had been ordered to start using a regulation II. *Gruppe* horizontal bar as well. Ever the individualists, however, the unit promptly opted to place its bar *ahead* of the fuselage cross, as seen here!

15

Bf 109F 'Black 10' of Leutnant Hans Strelow, *Staffelkapitän* 5./JG 51, Szolzy, c. February 1942

This 'Black 10', its temporary white winter camouflage well worn, was reportedly the mount of 5. *Staffel's* 19-year-old *Kapitän*, Hans Strelow. The 40 Soviet kills recorded on the rudder would seem to bear this out, as too does the addition of a small Knight's Cross and question mark after the 40th – 'where's my medal then?' has all the hallmarks of the impatience of youth! In fact, Strelow would have to wait until the following month, and 52 victories, before being decorated.

16

Fw 190A-3 'Black Double Chevron' of Hauptmann Heinrich Krafft, *Gruppenkommandeur* I./JG 51, Jesau/East Prussia, September 1942

In September 1942 I./JG 51 became the first *Gruppe* to return to the homeland to convert to Fw 190s. The *Kommandeur's* pristine A-3 already sports the unit's stylised 'Chamois on a mountain peak' emblem, but has not yet received its eastern front yellow theatre markings. 'Gaudi' Krafft would not long survive the return to Russia, being brought down by anti-aircraft fire on 14 December.

17

Fw 190A 'White 9' of Leutnant Oskar Romm, 1./JG 51, Vyazma, October 1942

Before commencing operations on the eastern front, many of I. *Gruppe's* early Focke-Wulfs received a coat of dark green camouflage – the better to blend in with Russia's large tracts of forest. They also wore their yellow fuselage band centred on the *Balkenkreuz*, a practice more commonly associated with JG 54. After claiming 76 Soviet kills with JG 51, 'Ossi' Romm became a successful *Sturm* pilot with IV./JG 3 in Defence of the Reich.

18

Bf 109G-2/trop 'Black 9' of 5./JG 51, Bizerta/Tunisia, November 1942

Ordered to break off their conversion to Focke-Wulfs, 4. and 5./JG 51 were instead equipped with brand new, desert finish Bf 109G-2/trops, before being transferred to Tunisia in November 1942. II./JG 51's 'weeping raven' (with its anachronistic Chamberlain umbrella) had finally disappeared. But note that the II. *Gruppe* horizontal bar had now edged even further forward – *ahead* of the machine's individual number.

19

Bf 109G-2/trop 'White 4' of Leutnant Günther Eggebrecht, 6./JG 51, Tunis/El-Aouina, December 1942

Shortly after arriving in North Africa, II./JG 51's vacant 6. *Staffel* slot was filled by redesignating 3./JG 1 (already in-theatre, and also equipped with G-2/trops). For a while, therefore, both 4. and 6. *Staffeln* were identified by white individual numbers. But the overly large size and style of the latter's numerals – together with the absence of a *Gruppe* horizontal bar – precluded any possible confusion.

20

Fw 190A-3 'Brown 9' of Oberleutnant Heinz Lange, *Staffelkapitän* 3./JG 51, Vyazma, December 1942

While II./JG 51 was confronting Anglo-American forces in Tunisia, the eastern front *Gruppen* were facing another Russian winter. 'Brown 9', in still fairly clean temporary white camouflage finish, was the mount of Heinz Lange, who would rise from his current position as *Kapitän* of 3. Staffel to become the *Geschwader's* sixth, and final, *Kommodore.*

21

Fw 190A-4 'White 10' of Unteroffizier Otto Gaiser, 10./JG 51, Bryansk, March 1943

Looking decidedly grubbier than Lange's machine, the

white winter camouflage on Otto Gaiser's 'White 10' shows evidence of hard use. Both Lange and Gaiser would be awarded the Knight's Cross in 1944 – for 70 and 74 victories respectively. But there the similarity ended, for Gaiser's decoration was posthumous (as was his promotion to leutnant) after he had been reported missing in action against four low-flying *Sturmoviks* near Lyuban on 22 January 1944.

22

Fw 190A-5 'Black Chevron and Triangle' of Major Erich Leie, *Gruppenkommandeur* I./JG 51, Orel, May 1943

Back to the dark green hues of summer for this *Kommandeur's* aircraft, albeit now minus the *Geschwader* badge on the cowling and with the yellow theatre band transferred to the aft fuselage position (compare with profile 17). Already a 43-victory Channel front *Experte* with JG 2 'Richthofen', Leie added a further 71 kills in the east after assuming command of I./JG 51. A final four whilst serving as *Kommodore* of JG 77 then took his overall total to 118 (some sources quote 122), before he was killed in action over Czechoslovakia on 7 March 1945.

23

Fw 190A-4 'Black 4' of 8./JG 51, Orel, July 1943

Two 'Black 4s' appeared on 8. *Staffel's* casualty lists during the opening rounds of *Zitadelle.* The first was forced-landed by Feldwebel Walter Bracke after a clash with Soviet LaGG-3s on 5 July. The second, reconstructed here from drawings and descriptions, was the machine in which Oberfeldwebel Hubert Strassl flew his last mission three days later. Strassl received a posthumous Knight's Cross for his successes at Kursk.

24

Hs 129B 'White 5' of Pz.J.St/JG 51, Southern Sector, August 1943

JG 51 was unique among eastern front *Jagdgeschwader* in having its own Hs 129-equipped anti-tank *Staffel* (although the unit rarely operated under the direct control of its parent *Stab*). Officially designated 10.(Pz)/JG 51, but more commonly referred to as the *Panzerjäger-Staffel* (Pz.J.St = anti-tank squadron), the unit's aircraft were identified in fighter style by white *numerals*, rather than the coloured letters employed by dedicated ground-attack *Staffeln.*

25

Fw 190A-6 'Black 8 and Bars' of *Stabsstaffel* JG 51, Bobruisk, Winter 1943-44

Another unit unique to JG 51 was its *Stabsstaffel* (not to be confused with the *Geschwaderstab* – i.e. HQ Flight – common to all *Jagdgeschwader*). This was formed from the original 6. *Staffel*, which was the only part of II./JG 51 to complete conversion to the Fw 190 after the remainder of the *Gruppe* had reverted to Bf 109s and been sent to Tunisia. The *Stabsstaffel's* markings consisted of a black numeral plus horizontal bars (the forward one pointed) on either side of the fuselage cross as seen here on this winter-camouflaged machine.

26

Fw 190A-6 'White 14' of Oberfeldwebel Günther Josten, 1./JG 51, Orsha, March 1944

Less comprehensively covered in white winter camouflage paint than the example above, but perhaps all the more effective for that now that the spring thaw was about to set in, this roughly daubed 'White 14' was the mount of recent Knight's Cross recipient Oberfeldwebel Günther Josten. Never once shot down throughout all his 420 operational missions, Oberleutnant Josten ended the war with 178 confirmed victories.

27

Bf 109G-6 'White 9' of Oberfeldwebel Günther Josten, 1./JG 51, Bobruisk, April 1944

By the beginning of April I./JG 51's conversion from Fw 190s back on to the Bf 109, begun late in February, was complete. This is Günther Josten's brand new G-6, resplendent in its pristine dapple grey factory finish with eastern front yellow theatre markings comprising spinner, aft fuselage band and underwing tips (inboard as far as the cross). Note also the black paint applied to the wingroot area to hide unsightly exhaust staining.

28

Bf 109G-6 'Red 13' of Leutnant Götz Bergmann, 5./JG 51, Gadurra/Rhodes, July 1944

The only one of JG 51's four *Gruppen* to remain on Bf 109s throughout the war, II./JG 51 continued to plough its own furrow in terms of markings. Note the horizontal *Gruppe* bar still positioned defiantly *ahead* of the aircraft numeral, in contravention of regulations, and also the two small emblems immediately above it – that on the left the new *Gruppe* shield, that on the right the *Geschwader* badge. 'Red 13' was the usual mount of Götz Bergmann, the leader of the *Kommando Rhodos* (Rhodes detachment).

29

Bf 109G-6 'Black Chevron Triangle' of Major Karl Rammelt, *Gruppenkommandeur* II./JG 51, Nis/Yugoslavia, circa August 1944

The man who introduced II. *Gruppe's* new badge, which resurrected the unit's original 'weeping raven' device as a tiny decoration on the handle of a stiletto shown piercing the insignia of the *Gruppe's* four wartime opponents (see *Jagdgeschwader* Heraldry, figure 5), was *Kommandeur* Karl Rammelt. Although not visible here, the shield was worn on the right hand side of the engine cowling in place of the *Geschwader* badge. As well as the 32 victory bars on the white formation leader's rudder, note the 'spiked club' personal insignia below the cockpit. This was not Rammelt's doing, but the work of an unknown hand that reportedly appeared on his machine overnight. Its significance is not known . . . could the *Kommandeur* really have been *that* hard a taskmaster?!

30

Fw 190A-9 'Black 15' of 14./JG 51, Garz/Usedom, April 1945

When it came to re-equipment IV./JG 51 went through more than most. The last *Gruppe* of the *Geschwader* to receive Fw 190s, it then became the first to convert back onto the Bf 109 (in the immediate aftermath of *Zitadelle*), only to start taking delivery of Focke-Wulfs again towards war's end. This blown canopy A-9 is an example of the latter. Note the 'wavy line' IV. *Gruppe* insignia which had by now replaced the small aft fuselage cross.

31

Bf 109G-10 'White 14' of Hauptmann Waldemar Wagler, 15./JG 51, Garz/Usedom, April 1945

A reflection of the chaotic conditions during the final days of the war, on 24 April Hauptmann Waldemar Wagler, a member of 15. *Staffel*, was ordered to lead two dozen G-10s culled from other units (hence the unknown II. *Gruppe* markings shown here) from Garz to Junkertroylhof, in isolated East Prussia, to reinforce III./JG 51. His take-off delayed, Wagler set off later than the others and ended up not in East Prussia, but at Rinkaby airfield, in southern Sweden.

32

Fw 190D-9 'White 11' of 13./JG 51, Flensburg, May 1945

In mid-April 1945 – with the end of the war only three weeks away – IV./JG 51 received at least six Fw 190D-9 'Long Noses'. After briefly operating with 13. and 14. *Staffeln*, all but one or two of these machines are believed to have been flown to Flensburg on 2 May to await surrender to British forces.

BIBLIOGRAPHY

ADERS, GEBHARD / HELD, WERNER, *Jagdgeschwader 51 Mölders.* Motorbuch Verlag, Stuttgart, 1985

CARELL, PAUL, *Unternehmen Barbarossa.* Ullstein, Frankfurt/M., 1963

CARELL, PAUL, *Verbrannte Erde.* Ullstein, Frankfurt/M., 1966

CONSTABLE, TREVOR J and TOLIVER, COL RAYMOND F, *Horrido! Fighter Aces of the Luftwaffe.* Macmillan, New York, 1968

FORELL, MAJ FRITZ von, *Mölders und seine Männer.* Steirische Verlagsanstalt, Graz, 1941

GUILLEN, SANTIAGO and CABALLERO, CARLOS, *Die fliegenden Verbände der Blauen Division.* VDM Heinz Nickel, Zweibrücken, 2000

HAMMEL, ERIC, *Air War Europe.* Pacifica Press, California, 1994

HELD, WERNER, *Die deutschen Jagdgeschwader im Russlandfeldzug.* Podzun-Pallas-Verlag, Friedberg, 1986

KUROWSKI, FRANZ, *Balkenkreuz und Roter Stern.* Podzun-Pallas-Verlag, Friedberg, 1984

MEILLER, HAFNER, *Flieger Feinde Kameraden.* Erich Pabel Verlag, Rastatt, 1962

MEINERT, KURT und TEUBER, REINHARD, *Die deutsche Luftwaffe 1939-1945.* Militär-Verlag Patzwall, Norderstedt, 1996

NOWARRA, HEINZ J, *Luftwaffen-Einsatz 'Barbarossa' 1941.* Podzun-Pallas-Verlag, Friedberg

OBERMAIER, ERNST, *Die Ritterkreuzträger der Luftwaffe 1939-1945: Band 1, Jagdflieger.* Verlag Dieter Hoffmann, Mainz, 1966

OBERMAIER, ERNST/HELD, WERNER, *Jagdflieger Oberst Werner Mölders.* Motorbuch Verlag, Stuttgart, 1986

OSTERKAMP, THEO, *Durch Höhen und Tiefen jagt ein Herz.* Kurt Vowinckel Verlag, heidelber, 1952

PLOCHER, Generalleutnant HERMANN, *The German Air Force versus Russia, 1942/1943 (2 vols).* Arno Press, New York, 1966/67

PRICE, ALFRED, *Focke-Wulf 190 at War.* Ian Allan Ltd, Shepperton, 1977

PRIEN, JOCHEN, et al., *Die Jagdfliegerverbände der Deutschen Luftwaffe 1934 bis 1945 (various vols).* struve-druck, Eutin, 2000

SHORES, CHRISTOPHER, et al., *Fighters over Tunisia.* Neville Spearman, London, 1975

STIPDONK, PAUL and MEYER, MICHAEL, *Das Jagdgeschwader 51 (Mölders).* VDM Heinz Nickel, Zweibrücken, 1996

ZENTNER, CHRISTIAN *Lexikon des Zweiten Weltkriegs.* Südwest Verlag, Munich, 1977

INDEX

References to illustrations are shown in **bold**. Plates are shown with page and caption locators in brackets.